Battlefield
of the
mind

C0-AZO-187

Battlefield
of the
mind

![image](for Kids)

JOYCE MEYER

with Karen Moore

WARNER
Faith®

NEW YORK BOSTON NASHVILLE

Scripture marked NIV is taken from the Holy Bible,
New International Version®. Copyright © 1973, 1978,
1984 International Bible Society. Used by permission
of Zondervan. All rights reserved.

Scripture marked NLT is taken from the Holy Bible, New
Living Translation copyright © 1996 by Tyndale Charitable
Trust. Used by permission of Tyndale House Publishers.

Scripture marked NCV is taken from the *New Century
Version* of the Holy Bible copyright © 1987, 1988, 1991
by Thomas Nelson Inc. All rights reserved.

If you purchase this book without a cover you should be
aware that this book may have been stolen property and
reported as "unsold and destroyed" to the publisher.
In such case neither the author nor the publisher has
received any payment for this "stripped book."

Copyright © 2006 by Joyce Meyer
All rights reserved.

Warner Faith
Hachette Book Group USA
1271 Avenue of the Americas
New York, NY 10020

Visit our Web site at www.warnerfaith.com.

Warner Faith and the "W" logo are trademarks of Time Warner Inc.
or an affiliated company. Used under license by Hachette Book
Group USA, which is not affiliated with Time Warner Inc.

Printed in the United States of America

First Edition: June 2006

10   9   8   7   6   5   4   3   2

Library of Congress Cataloging-in-Publication Data
Meyer, Joyce.
Battlefield of the mind for kids / Joyce Meyer,
with Karen Moore.—1st ed.
p.   cm.
ISBN-13: 978-0-446-69125-3
ISBN-10: 0-446-69125-9
1. Christian children—Religious life.   2. Thought and thinking—
Religious aspects—Christianity.   3. Spiritual warfare—Juvenile
literature.   I. Moore, Karen Ann, 1950–   II. Title.
BV4571.3.M49   2006
248.8'2—dc22   2005035537

Illustrations by Brian Byers

contents

Battlefield
of the
mind
for Kids

Chapter 1

You've Got Another Think Coming!

Figuring out what you really think is not an easy job. In fact, even when you think you know what you think, you may be surprised sometimes to find out you don't really think *that* at all. Sometimes you think something because you have a friend who thinks it, and you agree because that's part of what makes you friends.

1

For example, if your friend's favorite color is purple, you might both agree to have that be your favorite color and wear it every chance you get. Later, though, you might see something orange and love it and begin to wonder if maybe orange is really your favorite color. If you tell your friend that orange is your favorite color, then you've begun in a simple way to realize what it means to think for yourself.

It's good to have people who agree with the way you think. It's an even better idea to know *why* you think as you do. If you're not really sure what you think, or you've been thinking some very odd things that may not be true at all, then "you've got another think coming." God has a plan to help you discover how to think more clearly.

In Philippians 4:8, God gave us some great examples of things to think about. We're told, "Think about the things that are good and worthy of praise. Think about the things that are true and honorable and right and pure and beautiful and respected." The author goes on to say that if we do that, then the God who gives peace will be with us.

"Well, what do you think?" Don't your friends ask you that all the time? From picking out a movie to talking about favorite music groups, your friends care about what you think. When it comes to making choices of any kind, it's helpful to understand why you choose what you do. Those choices come from how you think!

Getting Your Thoughts in Shape

How do you shape up your thoughts or even shake out your thoughts so you can see which ones are really yours? Make a list for yourself right now. Write down the names of the people or things in your life that make a difference in how you think. Did you list athletes, or actors, or maybe a character in a book you read? Did you list your best friend, your sister, or maybe your mom? Perhaps you listed your pastor, or a Bible hero. From TV shows, to music groups, to church, family, and friends, everyone is part of the process that determines how you think today.

If you want to think good and worthy thoughts, those you might even be grateful for, how does that change the picture? Think about your goals for getting good grades, or becoming more active in your church group, or helping a friend do a good deed. How are your thoughts bombarded from the outside?

Getting Good Grades

Let's use getting an *A* in English as your goal. If you're good at English, this could be an easy goal and you might jump right to the *A* grade and add some kudos (praise) with chocolate chips. But, if you're not good at English and you still set this goal, how will your thoughts affect your hope of achieving an *A*?

First, you read something in the paper about athletes being paid millions of dollars to play a game, even though they barely got through school. The chances are very small that these millionaires got *A*'s in English. You then begin to think that English is not so important.

Then, your best friend teases you about becoming a little too geeky or nerdy. Now that *A* is not looking so important. After that, you remember a time back in the second grade when you heard a teacher say your writing wasn't very good. Of course, the teacher was trying to teach you to use correct letter form, but you just remember the statement and that probably confirms to you that you can't get an *A* in English.

Or maybe you just watched *American Idol* and you think, "There must be another way to get ahead in the world without getting *A*'s in English"—and even your dad says he wasn't good in English, so you must not be. Now your mind is full of great excuses why getting an *A* is just impossible!

Will the *Real* You Please Stand *Up*!

The point is that all these things influence how you think. How can you decide then how to think and set good goals for yourself? How do you know the *real* you?

In my book, *Battlefield of the Mind*, that I wrote for adults, I help them create tools that will be useful in getting their minds straight. Let's make a mental tool kit and put some of these ideas into it.

■ **Read your Bible:** Well, that seems simple enough, but where do you start? Let's look at Romans 12:2: It says, "Do not change yourselves to be like the people of this world, but be changed within by a new way of thinking. Then you will be able to decide what God wants for you; you will know what is good and pleasing to him and what is perfect."

Okay, you read that, now let's look at it again. It says to not follow the crowd, not just make a choice because everyone else has, not think that agreeing with your friends when they aren't making a good choice is okay. Be yourself!

So, What Should You Do?

Let's think a moment about why you want to be like your friends. Usually, you want to be like other people because you admire them, or think they are cool, or think they're very special in some way. Those are fine reasons to want to be like someone else.

GO LOOK AT YOUR BIBLE!

But what if the person you admire decides to do something you don't agree with? What if your friend decides to smoke, for instance? You already know that you think smoking is gross and disgusting. You already know your parents would be upset if you smoked. But what if your friend says something like, "If you're really my friend, you won't tell anyone that I smoke and you'll smoke with me." What do you do then?

When you take the Bible's advice and look within yourself to discover what's true for you, it may mean disagreeing with your friend and even choosing to not be friends for a while.

BRAVO FOR YOU!

This would be you thinking in a new way, looking at what is right for you. Thinking that way helps you know clearly what God wants for you and helps you choose a way that will be good and pleasing to Him.

■ **Give yourself permission to think your own thoughts.** The Scriptures give us patience and encouragement so that we can have hope. When you hope to make good decisions and have good thoughts, this tool will help you every time.

■ **Give yourself an opportunity to think again.** After all, you've got another think coming! The good news about growing up and changing your thinking is that you can always think again. You have another chance to make a better choice than you did the last time. You've probably liked this idea when you decided to try lima beans, for instance, and discovered green beans really are much better. The same principle is at work in other parts of your life. You're never stuck with having to think only one way. With Jesus, you've always got another chance.

■ **Think about Jesus.** You may have heard the popular phrase, "What would Jesus do?" The Bible says that in another way. It says, "Think about Jesus' example" (Hebrews 12:3). When you're making a choice, do your best to imagine what you think Jesus might do or how He might act in the situation you're facing. Go back to your friend who started smoking and think about it through Jesus' eyes. What would He tell your friend? What would He tell you? Think about those things.

■ **Don't be willing to be led astray.** In Hebrews, there's a reminder to hold on to the things you were taught. Don't let strange teachings lead you astray, or take you down the wrong road. Your heart should be strengthened by God's grace (see Hebrews 13:9). In other words, you have the answer within you. God has already given you what you need.

Now you've got a pretty full toolbox. If you carry it with you wherever you go, it will help you think straight. It will help you out on the battlefield—in the schoolyard, in the classroom, and at the party at your friend's house. You need to keep in top condition if you're going to win this one, and being equipped is only part of the answer.

Let's move on and see what's showing up in those old thought balloons.

Chapter 2

Popping a Few Old Thought Balloons

S ometimes it's hard to figure out what you think well enough to put your right thinking into right actions! When our character had to decide whether to go to a movie with his friends or stay home and study for a science test, his first decision was to go to the movies. Why? He didn't want to disappoint his friends, and he didn't want to look like school was more important than them. What would they think? He just couldn't make up his mind what to do.

The battle for your mind and your thinking will go on your whole life, but it's going to feel especially crazy now while you're in school. Your mind will likely jump and hop and swerve in a hundred directions, leaving you almost dumbfounded about what you really think and feel and what your options are.

I call this having a "confused mind," and you probably
know what I mean. When your mind is confused, it not
only wanders all over the place looking for answers before it even knows the questions, it just doesn't know
how to figure out what is normal and how to focus on
the right direction. It's in a no-win situation because it
doesn't know, so it can't win. The Scriptures put it this
way in James 1:5–8: "If any of you needs wisdom, you
should ask God for it. He is generous and enjoys giving

SOMETIMES I THINK FIVE OR SIX THINGS . . . OH ME! to all people, so he will give you wisdom. But when you ask God, you must believe and not doubt. Anyone who doubts is like a wave in the sea, blown up and down by the wind. Such doubters are thinking two different things at the same time, and they cannot decide about anything they do."

Does that sound like you in any way? Do you ever think two different things at the same time and feel unable to decide what to do?

So, what do you do? According to James, you should ask God for wisdom. What is wisdom? It's help in great big capital letters . . . H E L P!! You tell God that you don't know what you should do in the situation you're in and you need help or wisdom to make a good choice.

Making Confusing Choices

Let's say you're confused about whether to go to a party or not. You know that the popular girl who is having the party is kind of boy-crazy. You know that she has an older brother who may crash the party with some of his friends, and if your mother knew that, she wouldn't agree to let you go at all. You think that maybe if she doesn't know about the older brother, it could be okay and you could still go to the party.

Your mind starts to spin its web of confusion, and before you know it, you're trapped like the victim of a spider as you try to decide what to do.

Let's pretend you're now reading someone else's story and you can choose your own ending to this situation. We'll set the story up and then you can choose ending number one, number two, or number three. Hey, you're not supposed to be confused yet.

The Story

"Mom, I've been invited to a party at my friend Shari's house. It's her birthday, and she's just having a few kids over for cake and board games. Will you be able to take me over on Friday night and pick me up? Is it okay if I go?"

"Will Shari's parents be home?" Mom asks.

"Oh sure, Mom. They're really nice people, and I'm sure you'd like them. Shari said you could call her mom about the party if you want to."

"Well, I guess that won't be necessary," Mom said with a smile. "You just go ahead and have a good time. I'll take you somewhere tomorrow to pick up a little birthday gift for her."

"Thanks, Mom. That would be great."

As Sally leaves the kitchen after talking with her mom, she remembers her concern about Shari's older brother showing up with older kids. She debates whether to tell her mom that part.

Sally goes up to her room and calls her friend Shari. She tells her that she'll be allowed to come to the birthday party, and her friend is pleased. Sally asks if Shari's parents will be there, and her friend says, "Well, no, they'll be out for part of the evening, but my older brother will be here, and he's eighteen, so it will be okay."

Sally hangs up the phone and decides . . .

Ending One:

Sally hangs up the phone and decides she'll just keep that information to herself. After all, what could go wrong? Her mom will never have to know.

Sally goes to the party, and all is fine until Shari's brother's friends start getting into the liquor cabinet and giving drinks to the younger kids. Things are starting to feel very uncomfortable, and Sally doesn't know quite what to do. Her friend Shari says she's being a baby for getting so upset. It's just a little drinking. When a ten-year-old girl passes out on the floor, Sally gets really scared and calls her mom to come and get her. Sally tells her mom she just wasn't feeling well and never says a word about what really happened.

Ending Two:

Sally hangs up the phone and decides that she'd better tell her mom that Shari's parents will not be at the party. She knows her mom would not be comfortable with her going under those circumstances, and she wouldn't feel right not letting her know.

"Mom," Sally says quietly, "I just found out that Shari's parents will be out for part of the evening while the birthday party is going on. She says her older brother, who is eighteen, will be there, though, to watch over things. Is it still okay for me to go?"

"Sally, I know how much you'd like to go to this party, but I don't feel good about a group of kids being in the house unsupervised. I don't think Shari's brother would be much help if someone became ill or got into any trouble. Would you mind if I call Shari's mother to discuss this before we decide?"

"Oh, that would be great. I'm sure Mrs. Peterson would be happy to talk with you about it."

Sally's mother calls Mrs. Peterson and finds out that they will actually only be missing about the first hour of the party. Along with her son, she's called her mother, Shari's grandmother, to also be there until she gets home.

Sally is allowed to go to the party with a clear conscience, and she has a good time.

Ending Three:

Sally hangs up the phone and decides she'd better tell her mom that Shari's parents won't be home, after all. When she does tell her mom, her mom says that there is no way Sally can go because she's just too young to go to an unsupervised party, and Shari's older brother doesn't qualify as a good parenting model.

Sally gets angry with her mother and decides to sneak out and go to the party anyway. She tells her mom she's staying overnight with another friend who was not allowed to go to the party. Her mom thinks that's a nice alternative choice and takes Sally to her friend Margie's house.

Margie and Sally go to the party, even though neither of them are really allowed to go. They see Pastor Jones out mowing his grass as they pass his house, and he waves at them. Sally feels a twinge of guilt.

They go to the party, and things seem fine at first until one kid gets mad at another one and starts a food fight. Before Sally knows what is happening, food is flying through the air, and pizza is sticking to the ceiling faster than Shari's brother can get things under control.

Sally feels really badly about the house and just as she's trying to convince Margie that they should get out of there, Shari's parents come home. They stop the party and call all the kids into the living room. They tell them that they will be calling all of their parents to set up times for each kid to come back and help clean up the mess. Sally's heart sinks.

Sally's Confused Mind

Why did Sally have a confused mind? Did she know the right thing to do?

TRUST GOD, NOT YOURSELF!

Sally knew in her heart of hearts what she should have done. She became confused when she tried to give herself reasons or excuses for thinking something other than what she knew was the truth. God did not give us a spirit of confusion (see 1 Corinthians 14:33), so we can know right away that confusion means the Lying One is somewhere nearby and is tempting us to do the wrong thing.

If you know what to do in your heart, that's God's Spirit trying to help you make a good choice. If you don't want to hear what God has to say, you can find some pretty easy excuses floating around in your brain, and they'll always give you permission to do the wrong thing. You need to pop those excuse balloons right away!

The Doubt Demon

Another way you can get a confused mind is when you walk in doubt instead of in truth or in joy or in love.

Doubt crops up like ants at a picnic anytime you leave the door open. Your job is to see it as quickly as possible and close that door again.

God gave you a tool to help you get rid of doubt. It's called the "measure of faith." This measure of faith is the specific amount of ability for you to be able to believe and trust in something or someone. When you feel happy and confident and everything is going your way, you are living large and feeling like God is totally cool and in control, and you don't have a doubt or a care in the world.

But when you are having a bad day, you just failed the math test, you didn't play well in gym, and you just discovered there were peas for lunch, doubt comes in and camps in your corner.

Doubt will play all kinds of mean tricks on you. It will let you believe that you deserved to fail that math test because you didn't study hard enough, and not only that, it will convince you that you will never be good at math— so why even try? It will hop up on your peanut-butter sandwich and remind you that you just never were much of an athlete, and of course, you didn't make the A-team in volleyball because you're just not good enough. Then it will dive into your chocolate milk and remind you that Mom is making liver and onions for dinner because she just doesn't care that much about you, either.

Doubt Is the Villain

Doubt wants to control your thoughts so that you will stop making so much effort to do the right thing or to become all that God knows you are meant to become. If doubt can hold you back right now while you're in the fifth grade, imagine the fun it can have when you get to high school!

What Can You Do?

So, what are you going to do? What tool do you have to get rid of doubt? Go back to your measure of faith. How big is it? If you've just got a nickel's worth of faith, you're not going to be strong enough to push the doubts away. You need to grow your faith, increase in wisdom, and praise God beyond measure so that you'll be stronger and better equipped to fight off doubt when it comes in.

First Peter 5:8–10 says this: "Control yourselves and be careful! The devil, your enemy, goes around like a roaring lion looking for someone to eat. Refuse to give in to him by standing strong in your faith. You know that your Christian family all over the world is having the same kinds of suffering . . . God who gives all grace, will make everything right. He will make you strong and support you and keep you from falling."

Get out your measuring stick. How strong is your faith today? Pop those demon doubt balloons now.

A Sleepy Mind

When you feel sleepy, you're not especially interested in what is going on around you. You may not be able to pay attention in English class, you may not be able to hear the pastor as he delivers his sermon for the week, or you may not care too much about what your best friend is saying right that second. Being sleepy means you're not alert.

I call this condition a "passive mind." That means you just don't have anything much going on and you're not alert. Sometimes you are sleepy, and I'm not talking about being just plain tired from a long day. I'm talking about not keeping on the alert for the enemy and not being on the alert for what God wants you to know. You have to watch out for the things that will fill up those empty spaces in your head. When your head is empty, it's easy to fill it up with all kinds of lousy thoughts.

What Can You Do to Wake Up?

You can be sure that your mind is full of good thoughts. When good thoughts are cramming your brain, there's no room for nasty thoughts to hang out. They try to get in, and they see the God Squad at work in there and they just don't bother sticking around. Your best tool is to study the Word of God and pray.

You might think it's okay to **NOT** do those things and stay sleepy about them as long as you're not getting into any trouble or doing anything that might be considered wrong. But are you? If you think that you're not doing anything wrong when you're not doing anything, you might want to think again.

Sometimes problems march right into your head and stick around simply because they can see that nothing else is going on. It's easy for them to start playing games in your mind because you've given them a whole lot of space to do so.

Why Does Reading the Bible Help?

Ephesians 6:10–13 says this: "Finally, be strong in the Lord and in his great power. Put on the full armor of God so that you can fight against the devil's evil tricks. Our fight is not against people on earth but against the rulers and authorities and powers of this world's darkness, against the spiritual powers of evil in the heavenly world. That is why you need to put on God's full armor. Then on the day of evil you will be able to stand strong."

Reading the Bible is part of putting on your armor, or your protective suit, so that you know how to fight off the evil thoughts that may come your way. When you're sleepy, you're not a very good fighter. You're not very strong or alert. The Scriptures will give you tools to fight with.

What Is Prayer, and How Can It Help the Way You Think?

You've probably been saying certain kinds of prayers since you were a little kid. You've said prayers at night, perhaps with your parents, and you've said prayers at dinner. Now and then, you may have uttered a prayer of thanks when you did better on a test than you thought you would. By now you know that there are lots of ways to pray and different kinds of prayers.

As you keep growing, it's understandable that a lot of your prayers will be in the form of requests, asking God's help with school or family matters or friends. Those are great prayers.

Some of your prayers may be gratitude prayers, where you thank God for the good things in your life. The kind of prayer we want to talk about, though, is the kind that helps shape how you think.

Asking for God's Will

You come to God in this kind of prayer specifically to see if you can line up your thinking with His plans for your life. You're really putting yourself aside and asking that only God's will be done. That's a very grown-up prayer, and many adults even have trouble with that one. If you want to learn to think according to God's will and purpose for your life, though, this is a great prayer to offer.

Let's find an example of this kind of prayer.

The first thing you have to know is that you won't line up with God's plans and thoughts for your life by looking in the paper or anywhere else outside of yourself. In fact, you need to look inside yourself and check in with your heart to see how you really feel about what you want to pray about.

This kind of heart-to-heart prayer is one of the most special prayers you can pray. This one tells God that you're serious about getting the very best answer possible and that you really want to think more like Jesus. This one says you want your thoughts to be right, and you want to think as clearly as possible.

Talking to God

When you talk to God
You're sure to find
He'll give you joy
And peace of mind.
He'll hear your thoughts
And clear the way
To care for needs
You have today.

Here's an example of the kind of prayer we're talking about. See what Joe decides to do.

Joe just found out at dinnertime that his dad's company is being transferred to another city. He and his family will have to move to a new town in one month. Joe is not happy. In fact, he's mad. He's in the marching band at school and is part of the debate team, and he's not ready in any way to leave his friends. He just plain doesn't want to go.

He told his dad and mom that he thought this whole thing was lousy. After yelling as he left the dinner table that he wasn't going to go and that was that, he found himself in his room sulking. After a while, his mom came upstairs and knocked on his door.

She told him she was sorry that they would have to move, but there really wasn't much else they could do since his dad's work was the main support for the family. Joe kept sulking, but as his mom was preparing to leave the room, she offered him one more suggestion. "Why don't you try talking it over with God?" she said.

Joe wasn't so sure at first that he really cared what God thought, but as the evening wore on, he decided he didn't really have much to lose. After all, come tomorrow, he'd have to tell all of his friends that he'd be moving nearly eight hours away by car. His first tries at prayer didn't go very well.

His anger kept getting in the way, and he'd find himself just asking God to change this whole thing so they could stay put. Still not feeling any better with prayers like that, he decided to stop being angry and just tell God what was in his heart.

At that point, Joe's prayers changed. His new prayer sounded something like this:

"Hi, God,

I'm not feeling very happy right now. My dad says we have to move to another city, and I know I'm going to miss my friends. If there's any way You can change things so we don't have to move, I'd sure like that. If You could help me get through this and even help the way I think about it, that would be good. I know You want the best for my whole family. Thanks for listening.

Amen."

Do you see what Joe did right? You can do this, too! This prayer shows Joe's effort to get his thinking lined up with God's thinking. It may take some time for him to do that, but he's made a start, and God will be sure to help him. He'll do the same thing for you.

Be sure to include prayers for "right thinking" in your toolbox.

Chapter 3

I Heard It through the Grapevine

What's all that stuff floating around the halls at school?

Did you ever play a game called *Telephone*, where one person whispers something into the ear of the person seated by them, and then they pass the same words along to the person next to them, and the original idea goes all around the room until the last person is supposed to say what the sentence was?

For example, I might start the game with something like, "Chocolate sauce is really great with ice cream, bananas, and mixed nuts." By the time it goes around the ten people in the chain, the person who tells us the sentence says something like, "The truck driver put on his brakes when he saw some ice so he wouldn't get creamed like a banana in a rut."

Sometimes you carry around things in your mind that you think someone said or you heard through the grapevine, and then you worry about it, and later on you find out it wasn't even true. You might even find out that by the time the gossip got to you, it had been stretched like a yard of bubble gum and it wasn't even what the person who started the whole thing said at all. The halls of school are a great environment for stuff like that.

This Thing Called Gossip

Let's look at something that goes on all the time at school . . . this thing called gossip. What if someone spreads gossip about you? How should you think about that? Then, too, what if someone tried to share gossip with you? What should you do about that?

Gossip is usually mean-spirited. Someone who starts gossip isn't usually singing the praises of someone else, although that could happen. Gossip is generally meant to bring somebody down or make them upset. Usually it happens when one kid is angry at another or jealous over something. Whatever the reason, it's a very nasty thing indeed, and it hurts many people.

The Bible says in Proverbs 18:8: "The words of a gossip are like tasty bits of food. People like to gobble them up."

In another proverb, it says, "The person who tells one side of a story seems right, until someone else comes and asks questions" (Proverbs 18:17).

Choices about Gossip

It's important for you to watch out for gossip, whatever form it takes. What choices do you have if someone gossips to you or about you?

For those of you who like sign number one on the next page . . . applause, applause. Tell someone who really is being mean-spirited and wants to say bad things about someone else that you're too busy thinking about more positive things. Suggesting that Jesus doesn't want to hear what they have to say should stop the gossipy person right in their tracks! Bravo!

For those of you who like sign number two . . . it's time to shift your thinking. Getting the details about something that probably isn't supposed to be passed around, especially if you intend to pass it on, as well, means you're not thinking with your heart.

It means that you've forgotten a *big* rule: "Do unto others as you would have them do unto you" comes to mind (see Matthew 7:12). You also need to remember that those who will talk about others *to* you will also talk *about you* to others.

For those of you who like sign number three on the previous page . . . kudos, as well. Standing up for a friend or someone whom you believe is being talked about unfairly is a good thing. After you stand up for the person in question, just be sure not to pass along the things you heard, even to your own good friends. Sometimes we pass gossip along just by sharing our "concern" for someone. You know, the kind of thing where you start out by saying, "Did you know that Mary is . . . ?" and now your friend knows something about Mary she didn't know before. Be careful of this kind of communication because it can pull you right into the gossip rut.

Practice a Mind-set Like Jesus

So, when someone comes near you with some tasty morsels of gossip, it's time to practice having a mind-set that is more like Jesus' mind-set. Before you know it, you'll discover that people will come to realize that you don't like to hear their gossip, and they'll stop trying to share it. The gossip then might be, "Don't bother telling Jack. He doesn't like to hear gossip. He's one of those Jesus people." That's okay, though. You don't mind being thought of as a Jesus kid, do you?

What If the Gossip Is about *You*?

Now, what if it's about you? Proverbs 26:20 says, "Without wood, a fire will go out, and without gossip, quarreling will stop." In other words, if you don't fan the flames or react in a way that makes people think what they've heard is right, it will soon go away. When whoever started gossip about you realizes that they really didn't get the result they hoped for, that of making you feel bad or look bad, they'll stop doing it. It simply won't be worth the effort for them to keep going. The fire will die out.

So, why is gossip so destructive? After all, what's the big deal about passing along something you heard about someone, even if you don't know whether or not it's true? Let's play a little game of truth or lies. Your job is to decide whether each of the following statements is true or false. Then you have to decide whether you buy into the statement or not. Ready?

Statement One:

If I want to be class president, I have to do whatever it takes to win. I can't worry about the other guy. My job is to be a winner.

Statement Two:

If I want to be popular, I have to do what the popular kids are doing, even if I don't really agree with them.

Statement Three:

If I share bad news about someone else, it makes me look better because I seem to be part of the in crowd.

THE BEST
WAY TO WIN

Being a Winner

So, all of you hoping to be class president, or part of the swim team, or anything else where you have to compete to get in, what do you say? Is it more important to win and not worry about the other guy? Do you just do whatever it takes, even if it isn't totally on the up-and-up?

What would popular gossip say to do? What would Jesus say to do? How should you think about it?

What Is Right Thinking?

You have to start with right thinking. You have to start with Jesus and a mind-set that can give you clear direction. Galatians 5:25–26 puts it this way: "We get our new life from the Spirit, so we should follow the Spirit. We must not be proud or make trouble with each other or be jealous of each other."

When you compete, do it fairly. Do everything based on your values and principles and what you believe you have to contribute to the team or to the group. Do it in a way that will make you feel God's blessing because you are acting according to His will and purpose for your life.

Be a Winner in God's Eyes

Do what it takes to be a winner in God's eyes, and you will come out on top every time. The good news is that you don't have to be a star to win with Him. You're already His light in the world. You're His success story every time you choose to be on His team.

Being Popular

It's great to be popular. It's nice to be someone whom everyone knows and wants to be with and invites over. It's great, or so it seems to everyone on the outside of the popularity cult. What's really happening on the inside? What's going on in the minds of those who want to look like they'd do anything to stay popular? Is it worth selling your soul?

Being popular means that you think you have power. You can get what you want, get other people to do what you want, feel important at school, and so on. When you're the popular person, you sometimes forget to be the person who also can think and act independently of the group.

The Trouble with Groupthink

Today, a lot of youth gangs exist in this country. They exist in part because kids have bought into the idea that certain members of the group have power, and that if they want to have any power, too, they have to be part of the gang. They believe that if the group does it, it must be all right. You know, it's the old thing about "if everyone is jumping or running or playing the fool, are you going to do that, too?"

It's All Wrong Thinking

The sad thing is that that kind of thinking is all wrong. Once you've become part of the gang and given up your ability to think for yourself, you've lost power. In fact, you've lost yourself and are in trouble in more ways than you think.

Galatians 6:1–5 reads: "If someone in your group does something wrong, you who are spiritual should go to that person and gently help make him right again. But be careful because you might be tempted to sin, too. By helping each other with your troubles, you truly obey the law of Christ. If anyone thinks he is important when he really is not, he is only fooling himself. Each person should judge his own actions and not compare himself with others. Then he can be proud for what he himself has done. Each person must be responsible for himself."

It's okay to be popular. It's okay to be well liked. But be liked for who you really are as a child of God. Be a leader in sharing your smile, your kindness, your friendship, and your beliefs with those around you. Telling the truth of who you are will give you the freedom to be yourself. When you don't agree with popular opinions, it's okay to say so. In fact, you *must* say so in order to be true to yourself.

Getting Out of the In Crowd!

We live in a world that rewards knowledge. Knowledge is power, or so we are told. If you know something that other people don't, you have an edge on them. That's the way the world thinks.

How Do You Think?

How do *you* think? What helps you know when it's better to be outside of the in crowd and not try so hard to get in? When you think about it, you've got the most powerful information the world has ever known. You've got the key to salvation and eternal life.

Your Greatest Weapon for the Battle

One of your greatest weapons is the Word. John 8:31 says: "So Jesus said to the Jews who believed in him, 'If you continue to obey my teaching, you are truly my followers. Then you will know the truth. And the truth will make you free.'"

You must get the knowledge of God's truth in you and renew your mind with His Word. If you want to be smart, to have knowledge, to know things, do so from the Word of God. Know Him, and you will have real power.

Get to Know Jesus

If you're not sure about this, get to know Jesus. If you don't know Jesus very well, ask your family or your pastor to tell you more about Him. He's your friend. He's ready to guide you anytime you ask for His help. He died for you. He loves you just as you are. Don't be fooled. Don't let anyone try to change your

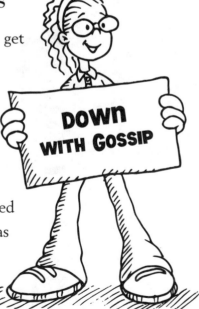

mind. Use the real wisdom that comes from prayer and reading your Bible, and keep your heart and mind on Christ Jesus.

If you want to share any news, share the Good News. You've got a calling to do that. Leave gossip and bad news and wrong thinking to someone else. You don't need it. Shine your light in the hallways at school.

Chapter 4

Whoa! Watch Out for Those Mind-Benders!

If you've watched any *Star Wars* movies or even any TV at all, you're aware of the battle that goes on all around us between good and evil. We're bombarded with things that can take our minds off track, and we don't need an encounter with Darth Vader to make it happen. Everything from magazines, to radio, to TV commercials attacks your thinking and makes it harder for you to figure out what's really good and what isn't.

So, How Do You Protect Your Mind?

It's important to protect your mind the same way you protect your body from outside invaders. You wash your hands before meals so that you don't get germs in your food that can harm your body. You've been taught safety rules and health rules and other rules to protect you when you go out into the world. Well, guess what? Your mind needs extra protection, too. It needs a rubber coating that will let some of the garbage that jumps into it bounce right back out again to keep you safely on track in your thinking. You need to wear the helmet of salvation everywhere you go.

You need to put on the whole armor of God.

Ephesians 6:11–17 says this:

Put on the full armor of God so that you can fight against the devil's evil tricks. Our fight is not against people on earth but against the rulers and authorities and the powers of this world's darkness, against the spiritual powers of evil in the heavenly world. That is why you need to put on God's full armor. . . . So stand strong, with the belt of truth tied around your waist and the protection of right living on your chest. On your feet wear the Good News of peace to help you stand strong. And also use the shield of faith with which you can stop all the burning arrows of the Evil One. Accept God's salvation as your helmet, and take the sword of the Spirit, which is the word of God.

Getting You All Bent Out of Shape

What are some of the things that might be heaped on you from mind-bending spirits? Let's look at a few examples and see what can be done to get them out of your head.

- Who do you think you are? You can't share your faith with anyone. They'll think you're a loony tune.
- What are you praying about passing a test for? Praying won't do you any good.
- You know you don't really have to get up to go to church. Your friends get to sleep in on Sunday morning.
- You don't really think your parents believe all this religious stuff, do you?

Mind-Bending Spirits

Mind-bending spirits want to confuse you into thinking that all the beliefs you have aren't really real. They want to make you feel that you just haven't caught up to the rest of the world. If you allow them to take over your thinking, you won't know what you believe anymore.

As a Christian, you have to decide what you are going to believe. Even though you're young, your faith is still strong, and you know things in your heart that haven't caught up fully to your head. You already have the seeds of truth planted inside you, and they'll keep growing your whole life if you nurture them.

So, What Should You Do?

You've got to pray those spirits away in the name of Jesus. You've got to say right out loud: "I come against false thoughts and mind-bending spirits in the name of Jesus." Those fiery darts will fall down around your feet and leave you alone. You'll be standing there with your shield of faith, and the devil's tricks won't be able to get near you. After all, you've got the full armor of God to protect you. You're better off than if you were in a rubber suit or walking around in a big bubble. In fact, a superhero could only wish to have what you have!

Thoughts about the Mind-Benders

■ **The truth is that you know exactly who you are.** You're a child of God, and you can share your faith because God will strengthen your spirit to do so. When the time is right for the person you share with, they'll grow in faith, too. That's the way it works. We're in a family that keeps reaching out to bring others into the family, too.

■ **Praying is the best weapon you have.** You should always feel free to pray about any situation. You can pray about a test, about a friend, about your family, and anything else that you feel is important to pray about. It's one of the side benefits of being connected to a loving Father.

■ **You belong in a church.** You may not always feel like getting up to go to church on a given Sunday morning. However, you've probably already discovered that when you do go, you feel so much better the rest of the day. Your heart is lighter, your spirit is more at peace, and the world looks a little bit better. Let your friends sleep in. You need to get to church!

■ **If your parents are Christians, they can help you.** You've been going to church with your parents since you were born. You were baptized and placed in their care so that they could help nurture your faith, as well as your mind and your body. Your parents may have been believers most of their lives, and nothing could change that. Your parents are your allies, and they are praying for you to grow and become even more of who God means for you to be. If this is true for you, then bless your parents and thank them for what they've given you.

In the future, when those mind-bending spirits start to nag you, lie to you, and make you feel all confused inside, remember this: You can send them packing by just shouting the name of Jesus right out loud. They can't stand even a moment of His glory. You have the truth within you, and it will set you free.

The Bible says this:

Let everyone see that you are gentle and kind. The Lord is coming soon. Do not worry about anything, but pray and ask God for everything you need, always giving thanks. And God's peace, which is so great we cannot understand it, will keep your hearts and minds in Christ Jesus. (Philippians 4:5–7)

Here's a little checklist that you can use to help you when you feel confused by mind-bending spirits. It gives you some Scripture references to read, some ideas to help clear your thinking, and some journaling space where you can jot down an idea or two of your own.

What to Do When the Mind-Benders Zap Your Thoughts Checklist

1. Pray: "Dear Jesus, please protect my thoughts and my mind. Please stand between me and any lies that might come into my head from mind-bending spirits."

2. Say out loud: "In the name of Jesus, I come against all mind-bending spirits."

3. Read Philippians 4:8–9. It's full of nice things to think about. It says: "Brothers and sisters, think about the things that are good and worthy of praise. Think about the things that are true and honorable and right and pure and beautiful and respected. Do what you learned and received from me, what I told you, and what you saw me do. And the God who gives peace will be with you."

4. Talk with your mother or father or a friend about any confusion you have.

5. Talk to your pastor or Sunday-school teacher about your thoughts.

6. Trust that God is with you all the time and will hear your prayers concerning anything on your heart and mind.

7. "Change your thoughts and you change your world," says Norman Vincent Peale.

8. When in need, repeat any of the steps on this list.

9. Write down your thoughts and concerns so you can pray about them. Put a journal beside your bed and write down your thoughts, the date, and what you prayed or what you felt concerned about. Then check back to discover how God answered your prayers. Be sure to include the answers in your journal, as well,

because they will renew and strengthen you when the need arises again.

10. Remember who you are, and focus your thoughts on Jesus.

Another Word about Media Mind-Benders

I just can't leave this chapter on mind-bending spirits without also talking about mind-bending media. I mentioned it at the beginning of this chapter, but I want to know that you realize your mind is being bombarded with a lot of information, and some of it is wrapped in very pretty packaging to get you to buy into it. Not all of that packaging is designed to bless your heart and mind and soul. You need to protect yourself from false advertising because it is thrown at you every day.

Let's just take a brief look at some of the ways this happens everywhere you turn. Who's out there sending you messages that are either totally not true, just true in certain situations, or meant to take away from what you believe about yourself? Here are a few of those sometimes dangerous mind-zappers.

■ **TV Commercials**—*Buy Me! Buy Me! Buy Me!* You know, the ones that make you feel like you just don't have the latest, greatest, and coolest stuff out there. They are designed to make you feel that if you just have their product, you'll be smarter, more popular, have more fun, and almost anything else you can think of. They make a lot of empty promises, and when you buy into the ad, you're sometimes in danger of thinking like *they* think, instead of thinking for yourself.

■ **Radio Commercials**—I know you don't listen to the radio nearly as much as kids did when I was growing up because you've got music on your digital music player, your computer, and everywhere else. But if you do tune in to a radio station, it can be pretty sad to hear the kinds of things the radio commentators say to you. Just be aware that they are paid to get as many people to listen to the program as they can, and so they often don't have a limit to what they will say to shock the listeners. You're better off sticking with

Christian radio if you're going to listen at all. There are some great Christian rock bands today.

■ **Magazine Ads**—You know the ones I mean. They have slick, glossy, beautiful photographs of toys, games, electronics, and they try to tell you what to wear, what to eat, and what to think. Again, they are designed to draw you in and get you to buy their products. Shopping is great, and it's fun, but just be sure you know why you're buying something. Don't buy into promises the product can't really deliver. They can airbrush anything to make it look good.

■ **Movies**—Your parents should always help you choose what you see at the movies, and fortunately, a lot of movies have ratings so that parents can do that job better. There's still a lot of stuff out there, though, that is rated as okay for you to see, but I can't help but wonder if you're getting the wrong message. Any movie you see needs to come with an added message that says, "This is just a movie . . . this is *not* real life." Sometimes movies can seem like real life, but they are not. If they try to make you compromise your values or your beliefs, they're sending the wrong message.

■ **Newspapers**—I don't know how much you look at the newspaper beyond the cartoon pages and the ads for new stuff, but it's good to know that every newspaper in the country is trying to serve a different audience, and it's slanted in one way or another to meet the needs of its readers. In other words, there's no un-biased reporting. That means they say what they believe the readers will want to see them print. The objective is to sell more newspapers. You have to be pretty smart to know when they are just giving you their opinion.

■ **Computer Ads**—Now you can hardly get away from ads wherever you go. You're no longer left with billboards and roadside signs and movie marquees, you have to deal with pop-ups that come onto your screen from all over the world. The good news and the bad news is that you can now get more information than any kid before you has ever been able to get. It can literally be mind-bending.

So, how do you protect your mind from the overload?
You go back to the checklist we included in this chapter. Start at the beginning, and go through it until your heart and mind feel safe again. Stay in shape, and you won't be led off the path. You can do it!

Chapter 5

Thinking About What You're Thinking About

I t might seem odd to remind you to "think about what you're thinking about," but it's an important idea. Here's why.

Taming the Traveling Mind

Believe it or not, your mind goes off on its own, and before you know it, it can be thinking about the strangest things. Why, with no reason at all, my mind can easily start thinking about things like chocolate and ice cream and what I'd like to be doing besides what I'm supposed to be doing. You know how it is when you're reading a book that you're not really interested in and somehow, before you can say "peanut butter," you're not even close to the pages of that book. Maybe that even happens to you sometimes when you're reading the Bible.

Help from the Bible

Well, speaking of the Bible, we've been given a few hints in God's Word as to what our minds should be thinking. Let's look at a few of them so that when your mind is off dancing to its own drummer, you can bring it back to the orchestra.

If you look into the Word of God, especially at Psalm 119, you get one idea of what to think about. Starting at verse 9, the psalmist says:

How can a young person live a pure life? By obeying your word. With all my heart I try to obey you. Don't let me *break your commands. I have taken your words to heart so I would not sin against you. L*ORD*, you should be praised. Teach me your demands. My lips will tell about all the laws you have spoken. I enjoy living by your rules as people enjoy great riches. I think about your orders and study your ways. I enjoy obeying your demands, and I will not forget your word. (verses 9–16)*

Let's take this passage apart and look at it more closely. The question that the psalmist is asking is the same one you might have: "How can a young person live a pure life?" (verse 9). That's a good question; in fact, it's a great question, and the answer comes right away.

How Can a Young Person Live a Pure Life?

"By obeying your word" (verse 9). By obeying God's Word! Wow!

There it is, and it seems simple enough, but it's a loaded response. We could go through example after example of what it means to obey God's Word, but we'll pick just a few of them to help you understand just what that means . . . to obey.

What If You Try and Fail?

But right away, the psalmist recognizes the problem. He says, "With all my heart I try to obey you" (verse 10). Isn't that the truth? Think about how hard you try to obey your parents and to live by the rules of your family. It's not always easy, is it? Sometimes you can't even do it. You may not have a rule book to help you study the fine print for the house rules, but you've got one when it comes to God's rules. Your Bible is right there for you to open anytime. Right?

You Ask God to Help You

Then the psalmist says, "Don't let me break your commands" (verse 10). Right away, he knows that it's not easy to keep the rules, and he's going to need help. He really wants to obey, but it's hard. Then the psalmist explains to God what he has already done to try to help him obey the rules. He says, "I have taken your words to heart so I would not sin against you" (verse 11).

Now, I call that thinking about what you're thinking about. What does it mean when you say you've taken someone's words to heart? When your mom tells you how smart you are, how much she believes in you, and how much she loves you, those are words you can take to heart. When you take those words to heart, you feel good. You know some important things about yourself. You know you're loved because you're a special person.

When You Take God's Word to Heart

When you take God's Word to heart, you know the same thing. He says He loves you, He wants you to believe in what He has designed you to become, and He knows you're able to learn more about Him and to work really hard at becoming all He means for you to become. So, that part makes the psalmist so happy, he says something equal to "Thanks a lot, God, and bring it on. I'm ready to learn what You've got for me."

He's really fired up with love for God now because he has the words in his heart and in his mind. He tells the Lord just what else he's willing to do. He says, "My lips will tell about all the laws you have spoken" (verse 13).

How Do You Show God You're Happy to Be His Kid?

Well, isn't that what you do when you're excited about something and you are happy? Don't you just want everybody to know what you know? Isn't that one of the ways you get great joy out of the love God has for you? You tell your friends. You tell almost anybody who will listen to you.

You Might Even Like the Rules

Finally, the psalmist tells God something else that's pretty important. He says, "I enjoy living by your rules as people enjoy great riches" (verse 14). Whew! Do you want to read that again? Can you imagine telling your mom how much you enjoy living by her rules or the house rules? Most kids, no matter what age, aren't too thrilled when there are rules to follow. The writer of this psalm not only loves the rules, but he loves them as much as some people enjoy being rich. Wow! Now, that's quite a mouthful. Think about that for a few moments.

Here's an Action You Can Take

We finish this portion of Psalm 119 with an action that the believer is telling God that he takes. This is something you can do, too. He says, "I think about your orders and study your ways. I enjoy obeying your demands and I will not forget your word" (verses 15–16).

This is the heart of thinking about what you're thinking about. Think about God's commands, study them, enjoy obeying them, and don't forget them.

That's *big*! Read it again:

- Think about God's commands.
- Study them.
- Obey them.
- Remember them.

Like the psalmist, it is important for you to think about what God has to say and what His rules are for your life. Thinking about what God wants you to know and understand takes a lot of time and a lot of study. It's not something you can put off until tomorrow. It's something to begin to know now, so that as you grow, God can add to your thoughts and your understanding to help you and to protect you out in the world.

A Couple of Stories You Already Know about Learning to Obey

More than a Whale's Tale . . . Our Man, Jonah!

This first story may sound a lot like Pinocchio's troubles when he ran away from his beloved father and creator,

Geppetto. In fact, it comes straight from the Bible and is found in the book of Jonah.

Here's the scene: The Lord spoke to Jonah and gave him specific instructions to go to Nineveh and preach against it because the people were being downright wicked and evil (see Jonah 1:1–2).

What did Jonah do? Well, he got right up and said, "Sure thing, Lord," and then took off in the opposite direction. For some reason, Jonah had the crazy notion that God couldn't tell where he was if he was running, so he bought a ticket on a ship and headed for a city called Tarshish (verse 3).

Imagine Jonah slipping onto the deck of that ship and thinking that he had outwitted the God of the universe and all would be well. Of course, we think this way too, sometimes, so we can't be too hard on Jonah.

Anyway, after Jonah found a bunk in the bottom of the ship and fell asleep, God began to create a storm that nearly shook the ship apart. All the people on the ship were praying to any god they could think of for help, but nothing seemed to be changing the climate. Finally, they drew straws to figure out who was at fault, and you guessed it, every straw said it was Jonah (verses 4–7).

The crew members asked him who he was and where he was going. Jonah had to confess that he had run away from the God of the universe. Since the sea didn't get any calmer, Jonah told them to throw him into the water, and then the sea would calm down. The men tried to be kind to him and hoped they could just row their ship back to the shore, but the seas would not quiet down. They finally begged God's forgiveness because they didn't want to kill Jonah, but they had no choice but to throw him into the sea. As soon as they did, the seas calmed down (verses 8–15).

Swooped Up by a Big Fish

God caused a big fish to come along and swallow Jonah, cowardly heart and all, and Jonah lived inside the fish for three days and three nights (verse 17). Of course, inside a fish, it might be hard to tell the days from the nights, and Jonah probably never had a piece of mackerel again, but we must go on. When you're inside the belly of a fish, you start thinking a lot about what you're doing, and that's exactly what Jonah did. He prayed. He begged for forgiveness. He thanked God for being with him even in that situation. He made a promise to obey God forever. So, God spoke to the fish and had the fish throw up Jonah back onto the dry land (see Jonah 3).

Coming Up for Air

Jonah must have been one great preacher for God to give him another chance to go and do what He wanted. Jonah didn't even have to prepare a message because God told him He would tell him what to say when he got there. So, the Bible says, *Jonah obeyed* (see 3:1–3).

Jonah walked partway through the city of Nineveh and told the people that after forty days (*Have you heard that number of days before?*), the city would be destroyed (see 3:4). A very interesting thing happened, though, and Jonah didn't expect it, but we can imagine that maybe God did.

The people believed God! They decided to stop eating and fast and wear clothes to show their sadness at how they had acted. Even the king of Nineveh did this. He commanded everyone to cry out to God for forgiveness. God then did a wonderful thing. He changed His mind. He did not destroy the city (see 3:5–10).

Jonah got mad. The funny thing is that Jonah was mad at God for forgiving the people of the city. He questioned God about being so willing to forgive them when they had been rotten people just a few days before. God was very patient with Jonah and gave him another example (see Jonah 4:1–4).

He made a plant grow to shade Jonah from the hot sun. Jonah was pleased to sit by the plant and enjoy its shade. The next day, though, God caused a worm to eat the plant and make it die. Then Jonah suffered in the blazing heat (see 4:6–8).

God tried to show Jonah that he cared more for the plant than he did for the people. But God cared for more than a hundred twenty thousand people in Nineveh, and Jonah was His answer to do so (see 4:10–11).

Isn't it good to obey God? When you're thinking about the Word of God and how you can use it to help you want to obey Him, remember Jonah. Jonah learned the hard way that his own ideas were all wet. You need to pay attention when things around you start to smell fishy.

Another Tale of Obedience

If You Can't Take the Heat, Stay Out of the Furnace

Three guys who could have been a rock group, but weren't, were Shadrach, Meshach, and Abednego. They were appointed by King Nebuchadnezzar to be leaders over Babylon. They were friends of Daniel, who helped the king interpret his dreams (see Daniel 1–2).

Though King Neb (*Do you mind if we shorten his name just for this story?*) believed somewhat in the God of Daniel, he wasn't totally sold on Him just yet as the story begins. In fact, King Neb had a great big statue (perhaps of himself, the Bible doesn't really say) made out of gold and ninety feet high that he set up in a pretty clear place in Babylon for everyone to see (see Daniel 3:1). He was so pleased with this work that he sent out his royal messengers to tell people this news: "Anyone who doesn't bow down and worship will immediately be thrown into a blazing furnace" (Daniel 3:6).

Bowing to Gold Statues

Now that was serious, and people everywhere were falling to their knees. Some Babylonians, who were kind of gossipy and had a grudge against Shadrach, Meshach, and

Abednego, wanted to make trouble. They told King Neb that some of his very own men weren't playing according to the rules. They made the king agree to punish his own leaders (see 3:8–12).

Another Chance?

Because King Neb really liked these three guys, he tried to give them another chance. He begged them to bow down to the statue and then they could all go home. The king was sure that no god could save them from the fiery furnace, and he figured they would just have to do what he asked (see 3:13–15).

Things Heat Up

However, they answered like this because they were all about obeying God: "Nebuchadnezzar, we do not need to defend ourselves to you. If you throw us into the blazing furnace, the God we serve is able to save us from the furnace. He will save us from your power, O king. But even if God does not save us, we want you, O king, to know this: We will not serve your gods or worship the gold statue you have set up" (Daniel 3:16–18).

Well, that was a bit hard for the king to hear. He got hopping mad and told the furnace fire-builders to increase the heat by seven times the normal heat. He had his soldiers tie up Shadrach, Meshach, and Abednego and throw them into the furnace. The flames were so hot, the men who threw them into the furnace were killed instantly (see 3:19–22).

The King's Surprise

After the three men had been dropped into the furnace, King Neb looked in to see how things were going. To his surprise, the three men were no longer tied up, and a fourth man was with them. They all looked fine. The king went to the opening of the furnace and called the men to come out (see 3:23–26).

Not Even Lightly Toasted

The three men came out. Their clothes weren't burned, their hair wasn't burned, why, they didn't even smell like smoke! Now, what's up with that? King Neb became excited and started praising God. He was awed that the three men had obeyed their God, disobeyed him, and their lives had been spared. He did the best thing a king could do then—he promoted the three men to even higher positions in his kingdom (see 3:26–30).

What Can We Get From this Story?

Most of the time, if we don't obey God, it won't be a life-or-death matter. Or is it? When you obey God, you know in your heart of hearts that you feel blessed and good and you understand what a special relationship you have. When you don't obey God, you want to hide like Jonah or get behind the bushes like Adam and Eve did. In other words, obeying God brings a better life for you.

Getting back to thinking about what you're thinking about, then, these stories also show this. Jonah thought he had a better idea than God, and even after he ran away and God saved him, he still argued with God's decision in the end. If you think about that, you might decide that it's a better idea to do what God asks you to do right up front before you have to handle a shipwreck.

Shadrach, Meshach, and Abednego help you to see that even when things appear to be all out of whack, if you can keep trusting God to help you and believe that He will help you, your beliefs and thoughts will prevail. You could never stand up and state your beliefs as clearly as they did, if your thoughts had not been focused on those truths for a long time. These were men who lived according to God's will and purpose.

Back to Studying the Word

You'll get from your own study of the Word whatever you put into it. The more you study, the more you'll understand. The more you understand, the more power you'll have to face the tests and problems of the world.

The basic idea is that if you want to do what the Word

of God says, you must spend time thinking about it. Romans 12:2 puts it like this: "Do not change yourselves to be like the people of this world, but be changed within by a new way of thinking. Then you will be able to decide what God wants for you; you will know what is good and pleasing to him and what is perfect."

Keep your eyes on the goal!

Chapter 6

Who's Minding Your Mind?

O kay, everybody out on the floor and give me fifty push-ups. Now, come on, I want the real thing. Let's go! Up, down, up, down! What? Getting winded already? You need to put your heart into it. Give it a little spirit!

When you exercise, you don't get quite as much out of it if you don't put all of your body, your mind, and your spirit into it. If you have played any kind of sport, or practiced for anything from a school play to a piano recital, you know that you have to fully pay attention to what you're doing.

Learning about God and thinking about your life is the same deal. You have to pay attention. You have to give it some gusto. You have to practice and practice and prepare for the big moments when you might be called into the center circle. God is busy giving you tools to build you up and prepare you to be on His team. Let's look at some of the things that might keep your mind off the goal and distract you from the game.

Figuring Out If Your Thoughts Are Okay

One of the writers of the Bible was a follower of Jesus, and his name was Paul. He talked about having the "eyes of our hearts" opened and filled with light (see Ephesians 1:8 NLT).

Of course, you may remember that Paul was the guy who was against the followers of Jesus at the beginning. He was eager to destroy the Lord's followers, and as he headed to a city called Damascus to find people to punish for their beliefs, he had an amazing experience. It went something like this (see Acts 9:1–2).

Paul and a group of his men were heading down the road toward the city in the early evening. Suddenly a very bright light beamed down on him from above, and a voice called out to him. "Why are you persecuting Me?" (see 9:3–4).

Paul could hear the voice, but he couldn't see who was speaking to him because the light was so bright. He said, "Who are you?" (see verse 5).

Jesus answered him and told him who He was. He directed Paul to keep going into the city where he would be told what to do. When the beaming light disappeared, Paul discovered he was blind. His men had to help him go into the city (see verses 5–8).

Blind Eyes of the Heart

Before we go on and learn more of what happened to Paul, let's think about you and me. Are we ever blind to what God wants? Do we need a beam of light to shine on us so that we get what God wants us to know? Sometimes we are blind. Sometimes we can't see to save ourselves. In fact, Paul was in that place where he couldn't see "to save him."

Think about what it means when you can't see. You know how it is when you're looking for the match to one of your socks, or you're looking for your favorite CD and you know right where you put it, but can't see it? Finally, you ask your mom if she knows where it is, and it's so maddening because she always does and you just don't know how she does it.

Not finding your sock is one kind of blindness, but not having the eyes of your heart open, well, that's another. You can always get another pair of socks. You can't get another heart, and you can't get another mind to try to understand what God wants you to know. You have to be willing to look and discover those for yourself. You have to search as though your life depended on it, because it does. Your spiritual life is that important to God.

So, let's get back and find out what happened to Paul,

and then move forward about twenty centuries to find out what can happen to you.

Let There Be Light . . . in Paul's Eyes!

Now you can imagine that Paul was a bit spooked by what had happened to him on that road. One minute he's a man with a mission, heading down a road, ready to bash a few Christians. The next minute, he's caught in a major light beam from the sky, knocked to the ground, hears a voice identifying Himself as Jesus, and when the light goes away, his sight goes away, too, and he's suddenly in the dark about what just happened.

When you're in the dark, you look to find the light switch as quickly as possible, and you can be sure, Paul was hoping for something like that, too. When Paul got to Damascus, he stayed three days in the dark, praying and waiting for something to happen. He didn't eat or drink, either.

Meanwhile . . . on the Other Side of Town . . .

On the other side of town, God was busy preparing the answer to Paul's prayers to restore his sight. God had already talked to one of His servants, a guy named Ananias. God told Ananias that he needed to go visit Paul (who at that point was still named Saul, but God was about to change his name, as well as his mission) and heal his blindness (see 9:10–12).

Now, that might sound like a nice thing for God to ask you to do. However, Ananias had to have some special "eyes of the heart" to understand why God would ask this of him. He had heard about Paul's reputation to do nasty things to Christians. Don't think he wasn't just a bit nervous about meeting this Paul person (see 9:13–14).

God reassured Ananias that it would all be okay because He had some new plans for Paul. So Ananias went (see 9:15–17).

When Ananias found Paul, he told him that Jesus sent him, and he even remarked about knowing that Jesus appeared to Paul on the road. That had to make Paul pretty sure this guy knew what he was doing because Paul hadn't told anybody what happened to him (see 9:17).

Ananias told Paul that God sent him to help Paul get his sight back and to fill him with the Holy Spirit. At the touch of Ananias, something like scales fell from Paul's eyes. He saw the light. He got baptized and ate some food (see 9:18–19).

What Does Paul's Story Have to Do With You?

You can read Paul's story for yourself in the ninth chapter of Acts. His story is a great example of what it means to be blind. Paul was a smart man. He went to the best schools. He had money. He had power. If he lived today, he'd have the big house on the hill with the best surround-sound system and all the latest computer gadgets, because he knew what was going on. His friends would have said that he was really the guy to know. His future looked bright.

Little did he know how bright! The point is that you can have the best DVD collection, or the nicest house on the block, or be the smartest kid in geography class, and still be blind. That's right. Your mind and spirit can still be disconnected. That's what Paul's story is about, and that's what your story is about. You need to connect the dots from all the stuff you've learned so far in school, and at home, and at church, and see if the eyes of your heart have been opened yet. You need to see if you get it.

Get what? Do you get that you are a child of God, and that He has a purpose for your life and a mission just for you? Do you get that the sooner you start on it, the more you can do for Him and the more light he can shine on you and help you fight off any of the darkness that ever tries to get around you.

You need to see the light just like Paul did. You need to have ways for your mind, the part of you that is totally smart, to catch up with your spirit, the part of you that is totally owned by God. According to the Bible, the mind and the spirit have to work together to understand this completely.

How Can Your Mind Help Your Spirit?

First of all, you have to know that sometimes your spirit is really working hard to help you understand things about God. So, even though the spirit is trying to help you live a better life, your mind can just be too busy to hear it and not catch on to what is happening.

Think of it like this. Think about when your math teacher was trying to explain square roots one more time and you were there listening, but your mind was off in a hundred other directions, so that the only thing "square" in the room as far as your mind was willing to think, was your teacher. Your mind was too busy to listen.

Add to your wandering mind the fact that your friend is trying to catch your attention. Your best friend is across the room trying to whisper something to you and mouthing every syllable so that you can understand what is being said. But the whole room is in an uproar, and for some reason, everyone is talking at once and you can't hear your neighbor, much less your friend across the room. Now imagine if you could hear the thoughts of every kid in the room. There's so much noise now, you could hardly hear yourself think. The only way God can get through to you is to turn a light on. He sends a blinding beam of light down to focus on you, because otherwise you might not be able to hear what His Spirit is trying to say.

If your mind is overloaded with thoughts of the day, with other kids' voices playing in your ears, along with what Mom said would be for dinner and what Dad said you should remember today, you're not going to be tuned in. In fact, it's amazing you can get your school-work done at all.

So, How Do You Hear God's Voice?

You get very, very quiet. You take a deep breath and pray. You listen.

Your mind should be at peace. It should be ready to listen, be alert, and be at rest. Your mind cannot go wandering.

We've talked a bit already about how you can be aware of a mind that wanders off. One thing you have to do is concentrate. Remember the preparation we talked about at the beginning of the chapter; when you're preparing to run a race, or do some exercise, you've got to concentrate. You've got to focus on the job at hand. Your mind needs that kind of focus all the time.

If you didn't get enough sleep last night, or if you've got worries on your mind, you might have trouble with this idea of focus. If you're reading the same page for the third time in your social-studies book, the chances are good you're not able to focus. Rest a little, and then try to concentrate more later.

Everybody daydreams now and then. We're not really talking about when that happens because sometimes it's important to just let your mind rest. We're talking about the fact that you can have some control over letting your mind wander off, and you can run after it and get it to come back before it gets too far away.

If your dog wanders off into the neighborhood, you go calling for him to come home. You don't want him to stray too far from your house. The same is true for you. Since your body is the temple of God, you need to be aware of what you're thinking all the time. If your mind wanders off, you need to call it back home.

What Kinds of Things Distract Your Mind?

Most kids will say they can easily do their homework in front of the television set with their headphones on with their favorite CD playing and still eat pizza and get an *A* on the paper they're writing. That's what they *say*. Maybe you're one of those who can do that. Maybe you're not. It's good to look at how easily you can be distracted, though, because maybe then you can stop those distractions right in their tracks.

See if you can put this list in the order of priority of

what you find most distracting. Number from ten to one on a piece of paper, and see if you can figure out the number one thing that distracts you when you're trying to focus on something you need to do.

Common Distractions

- Commercials on TV.
- Songs on the radio.
- Sister or brother who interrupts you.
- Ringing telephone.
- Cat jumping in your lap.
- Somebody outside mowing the lawn.
- Fire engine screaming down the street.
- Barking dog.
- Hunger.
- Ringing doorbell.

Look at your list and the order you put it in, and you should have some idea of what you need to do to find a more peaceful place to work when you have to concentrate. Think about the times when you want to pray. Do any of these things distract you then? If you can name those things that keep you from letting your mind be at peace, then you can work on ways to keep them from distracting you. You'll have a weapon to help you battle the whole mind-wandering issue.

The Wonder Years

Some of us never outgrow the wonder years. We wonder almost constantly about everything. We might even think of it as a tame version of worry. We wonder what will be for dinner. We wonder what the test will be like in English. We wonder if we'll have good friends all through life. We wonder if people really like us. We wonder if Mom will take us to the movies. We wonder about things all the time.

A healthy curiosity is a good thing when you're focused on doing a special research project on the life of bees, or what it takes to get a rocket up to the moon. You can wonder about those things if you're going to go off and begin to study about them so you can learn something. That kind of curiosity is what wondering should be all about. Most scientists start out by wondering about something.

But we're talking about a different kind of wondering here. We're talking about all those little things that set your mind in a tizzy because you can't really do anything about them or actually get the answers right away, and they're simply not in your control. When your mind gets lost in that kind of wondering, it is totally a waste of your time. You aren't going to get one answer anytime soon.

When Your Head Is Full of *You*!

When you're wondering about everything, you have a hard time making decisions, you feel confused, and you aren't able to hear anything God might be trying to tell you. Your head is too full of *you*! When your head vibrates with all the things you wonder about, it can't be calm enough to receive any guidance from the Holy Spirit. You need to stop all that wondering and calm your mind and pray. When you pray, you'll be able to get the answers you're seeking.

When you read what the Bible says in Mark 11:23–24, you'll see that Jesus did not say to His followers, "Whatever you ask for in prayer, *wonder* if you will get it." Instead, He said, "Whatever you ask for in prayer, *believe* that you will receive it—and you will!"

You need to be in the Believing Years!

Chapter 7

When the Best Grade You Can Get Is *Zero*!

Y ou work hard in school. You try to get *A*'s as often as you can by cramming your head full of ideas and facts and opinions. You do it in every class you take, and by the end of the day, your mind can be on overload. You might wonder if your brain will simply short-circuit.

As good as it is to get those *A*'s and to learn all that you can, sometimes it's even better for you to just take a break. Do a few somersaults, pop some popcorn, and rest. Go back to the beginning and take a deep breath. Going back to the beginning in this case means going back to your source of strength and inspiration and real knowledge. You can go all the way back to zero, where the only fact you need is your faith in Jesus Christ and His love for you. It's time for you to put on the mind of Christ.

"Oh sure," you're thinking. "That's not exactly easy. If that was a test, I'd probably fail."

Well, you're right. It's not easy, but it is something you can study up on and work on. In fact, there's a lot you can do.

All through this book, we've been talking about how you can make the kind of choices that will give you the right mind-set. Right choices lead to right thinking. Right thinking leads to Jesus. You've hung in there this far, so let's keep going, okay?

How Do You Put on the Mind of Christ?

First Corinthians 2:11–13 gives us part of the answer when it says: "No one knows the thoughts of God except the Spirit of God. Now we did not receive the spirit of the world, but we received the Spirit that is from God so that we can know all that God has given us. And we speak about these things, not with words taught us by human wisdom but with words taught us by the Spirit." Wow! What does that mean? It means that once we believe in Jesus, God gives us the Holy Spirit to come into our hearts and minds and help us understand more fully the things of God. If we didn't have Jesus, we wouldn't be able to understand the things of the Spirit. As we grow, we learn more from the Spirit, and we become more like Jesus. At least, that's the goal. Sure, it sounds easy enough, but let's keep going.

What Does It Mean to Really Put on the Mind of Christ?

Okay, I've brought the question back up again because the Bible verse told us what happens when we have the

Holy Spirit to help us understand the things of God and the ways that Jesus might think. How do we really do that?

First of all, we don't get an instant mind meld from some alien being where we're blissfully zapped and everything from then on comes out right. That would be nice, but it's not going to happen. We also don't get to drop a packet of good thoughts into some water, watch them fizz, drink them down, and suddenly be transformed. In fact, we don't get this mind of Christ quickly and easily at all. It's a lifelong process from being a kid to being an adult and having a mind that wants to keep learning and growing. All of us are working on it. All of us want to get more of what Jesus thinks and less of what we think.

Part of having a change of mind is about having a change of heart. When your heart is "in the right place," as we so often say, then you're more apt to do the right things. Let's look at some more Bible verses that speak about how our minds work.

Heart, Soul, and Mind

Jesus replied, "You must love the Lord your God with all your heart, all your soul, and all your mind" (Matthew 22:37 NLT).

What does it take to do anything with your heart, and your soul, and your mind?

What is your heart?

Your heart is your emotional center. It is the place where you feel deeply about the things that are important to you. It's the place where your mom and your dad and your family and friends live. It's the place where you have the deepest desires of what you want to become and what you want life to be about. You feel these things in your heart.

What is your soul?

Your soul is the essence of you that will live forever. It is the place where the Spirit of God lives within your being and connects to all the other aspects of you that surrender to the will of God. John of the Cross said, "The soul is in itself a most lovely and perfect image of God."

In other words, it's worth understanding, and you'll understand more about your soul as you continue to grow in Jesus.

What is your mind?

Your mind is the tool that God has created in you that gives you the power to think and react and look at life from all points of view. It is the keeper of your joy and your sorrow. It is the place where you get to know who you are and what you are to become. It is a part of your being that is continually in need of being renewed.

Now, put these three things together and add the idea

of love. Love with all your heart, all your soul, and all your mind. Well, that's a pretty *giant idea*! If you think about loving your mom or someone else you care about with this degree of focus, you will begin to discover where we're going here.

But wait, we still have to add the most important ingredient for this statement. *Who* are you to love? You're to love *God* with all your heart, all your soul, and all your mind. Now, try to imagine *that*!

The Things You Love

Think for a moment about the things you love. You love spaghetti, you love your dog, you love chocolate, you love music, and you love your best friend. Those things are pretty small in comparison to what Jesus is suggesting here. Those things we just named don't need all your heart and mind and soul. Only God needs that. We're looking at love in a whole new way. Maybe we could even guess that God wants you to love Him like this, because that's how He loves *you*!

Luke 10:27 puts it a little differently. It says,

Love the Lord your God with all your heart, all your soul, all your strength, and all your mind. Also, love your neighbor as you love yourself.

Luke even adds that you must love God with your physical body, as well, with "all your strength." Imagine having all this love for God and knowing that everything in you is tuned into this great love. What are you supposed to do with it? Inquiring minds want to know!

One of the answers given is this: You are to "love your neighbor as you love yourself." If you love your neighbor as yourself, it's a pretty sure thing that you have tried to put on the mind of Christ. You have learned how important it is to love with everything you've got and to put the needs of others before yourself. That's the goal. That's what God wants you to do.

One More Time . . . What Does It Mean to Love Your Neighbor?

You've been learning about loving your neighbor all your life. You learned to share your toys in nursery school. You learned to help out around the house and lend somebody a hand when you were needed. It's the same idea, except that it isn't a matter of doing it only when you feel like it. It's a matter of choosing that way of being and acting all the time. It's a matter of putting on the mind of Christ each day.

In Acts 2–4, the believers were getting their first experience of the Holy Spirit. This was a new thing for them and something really important happened to them. They were in love with the Lord and in love with each other.

"All the believers were of one heart and mind, and they felt that what they owned was not their own; they shared everything they had" (Acts 4:32 NLT). That passage goes on to say that people who owned houses and property sold them, so that they could bring the money back and share it with all those in need (see verse 34). That's a powerful way to be of one heart and mind. Taking care of all those in need would be "putting on the mind of Christ." Wouldn't that be an amazing thing to see?

So, How Can You Take Care of Your Neighbors?

- Ask if you can volunteer at church in the nursery or help the younger kids with a project.
- Help out with vacation Bible school.
- Research ways that kids can help in their local communities.
- Pray for others.
- Be a good citizen.
- Help out around the house.
- Hug the people in your family.

■ Help your mom at a soup kitchen.

■ See what you can clean out of your closet and give to someone less fortunate.

■ See if you have any old toys that you could give away.

■ Write notes to people you don't get to see often and let them know you care about them.

■ Get a pen pal through your church, either in the U.S. or in another country.

■ Ask your mom for some other ideas.

Be sure whatever you do, though, that you get your parents' permission before you start. These are just some ways that you can be a good neighbor and help others. I'm sure you know lots of other ways and that you're already sharing your special gifts. In those ways, you truly are "putting on the mind of Christ." You will find as you do for others your thinking about everything will be more in line with God's word.

Keeping a Positive Mind

Being a positive person is about having a positive mind-set, which is not the same as pretending to be happy all the time. Having a positive mind-set is really about how you choose to "see" the things that go on in your life. Let's look at an example.

Hurricane Closes the Disney Theme Park

Your family vacation has been set for months, and you're all heading for Disney World for spring break. You've been counting the days and saving your pennies and figuring out what you'll wear and what you'll say when you meet Mickey and Minnie. You're set to go! The day before you're supposed to take off, *Hurricane RuinEverything* comes through, and the park is forced to close. According to the news, they'll be closed for several days for repairs after the hurricane leaves the area. Your family will be given rain checks to come again whenever they choose.

What Will You Do When This Happens?

Whether you have a positive or a negative mind-set, you are expected to be disappointed about this. After all, you were looking forward to really having fun and getting away from your normal routine. No doubt, your parents are upset, too. That's a normal reaction.

But what you do with your disappointment after you've gotten through those first feelings of anger and sadness is the key. Let's look at some possible reactions. Take a look at Sulky, Zippy, and Sassy.

Sulky's Story

Why did that old hurricane have to come now? Why couldn't it ruineverything for somebody else? Why did it have to ruin the one fun thing I was going to get to do this whole year?!

Everything bad happens to me. My friends are already gone on their spring vacations, and now I don't have anyone to play with. Mom made me clean my

**room every day for weeks because we were going on
this trip, and now we're not even going.**

**I just hate my life. How come nothing good ever
happens to me?**

As you can see, Sulky took the whole incident and turned it into a personal defeat. Somehow, the whole world is down on Sulky, and this hurricane was part of some kind of plot to make his life miserable. Clearly, he's not meant to enjoy life, and everything is ruined. That's his mind-set. Is it doing him any good?

Zippy's Story

**Zippy was really disappointed when she heard that
her family would not be able to make the trip to
Florida. She looked at her packed bags and her pictures of Cinderella and all the characters she was
looking forward to seeing and thought about what
to do.**

**She looked through her book about all the things
you could see and do at Disney World and had an
idea. She'd make everybody in her family a special
pass for getting into the park. It would be a "hurricane-
can't-stop-us" pass, and they could pretend they
were playing in the park that very evening. After all, it**

would just be a few weeks before they would get to go for real.

Zippy set to work. She cut out pictures of rides and space stations and animals and characters and put them on pieces of cardboard. Then she put the name of each person in her family next to one of the pieces. She created a special invitation for each one to imagine what was going on there and to talk about the fun they would have in a few weeks when the park was open again.

Zippy took her work downstairs to share with her family. They all had fun as they talked about what they would do when they actually got to the park. Zippy helped her whole family feel better.

After all, a hurricane wasn't anybody's fault. Zippy wanted to help everyone feel better as soon as possible. What a difference a positive attitude makes!

Sassy's Story

Sassy didn't take the news of the hurricane well. She started out sulking a bit, but then she just got angry. Her anger made her feel worse and worse, and she took it out on everybody in the house.

"I don't believe the news," she told her dad. "I think we should just go anyway. It's probably not that bad."

"Planes can't even fly into the area right now, Sassy," her dad explained. "They really are having a hurricane. Don't worry, we'll still go in a few weeks when things get back to normal."

Sassy blew up. She stormed up the stairs, slammed her bedroom door, and started throwing things around in her room. Her mom came in to check on her, and Sassy just yelled at her at the top of her lungs. She didn't care what anyone had to say. She was angry, and she wanted them all to know it.

Sassy even shouted at the cat, who really didn't have anything to do with it, no matter how you looked at things.

It's pretty clear by these three examples what a difference a positive mind-set can make. No matter what comes your way to disappoint you—and disappointment will come your way a lot in life—you have to manage it. You have to create a way to think about it that makes it better and not worse.

How? Think Positive Thoughts

Since you're already aware of "putting on the mind of Christ," you have some idea of what it might mean to think in a positive way. You know for sure that God is positive.

You know that partly because you learned from the time you were a little kid that God is love. Love is positive. You get the picture.

What can you do to add a positive spin to the things that happen in your life? You can:

- Look for the good in any situation.
- Remember that you can change your mind and your attitude.
- Ask God for help.
- Look for something better to come along.
- Know that God wants what is best for you.

- Know that God cares when you're disappointed.
- Look for ways to solve a problem rather than add to it.
- Let people you love help you.
- Help people you love.
- Eat pizza.
- Keep a journal so that you can remember what you did that was helpful in case this ever happens again.
- Choose to make the best of things.
- Add your own ideas.

You can see that even though you may not be able to control the weather or hurricanes or even smaller events in your life, you *can* control how you choose to look at them. Asking yourself how Jesus would handle the situation could be a good place to start. You can always be a bright spot if you choose to be positive in the storms that come along in your life.

You see, every time something blows in on you, you can always go back to the beginning, the place where Jesus will meet you and help you get through what's ahead. You never have to face life's challenges alone.

Chapter 8

Doubt and Depression Belong in the Dumpster

Two of the biggest demons that your mind will ever battle are doubt and depression. Both of them will slink around you, waiting for a chance to break into your mind and make you believe all kinds of things that just aren't true. Think of them both as big dumb thugs who have no business being in your life. They never are part of God's plan for you, and they will have a hard time ever bothering you if you have put on the mind of Christ.

So, How Do You Battle the Doubt Demon?

You can start by writing this little poem on a piece of paper and hanging it on your wall.

Doubt sees the obstacles,
Faith sees the way;
Doubt sees the blackest night,
Faith sees the day;
Doubt dreads to take a step,
Faith soars on high;
Doubt questions, "Who believes?"
Faith answers, "I!"

I don't believe that God ever puts doubt in our minds. That's a trick of a demon. The Bible says that God gives every man (and every kid) a "measure of faith." Romans 12:3 says, "Do not think you are better than you are. You must decide who you really are by the amount of faith God has given you."

Earlier in the chapter, Paul wrote: "Don't copy the behavior and customs of this world, but let God transform you into a new person by changing the way you think" (verse 2 NLT).

So, the question is, will you let God transform your

thinking, or will you let a doubt demon in your mind to tell you what you can and cannot do? This is a great thing to learn now because it will help you all your life. Doubt is *not* from God.

The funny part is this: Doubt demons are assigned to work on you *because* you have faith. If you didn't have faith, they'd probably leave you alone. It's your faith they try to attack. God put the faith in your heart. Don't let anything or anyone take it away!

How Can You Do Battle with Doubt Demons?

Read, Study, and Speak the Word

Doubt demons swoop down on you any time you're tired or worried or simply not at your best. Usually your spirits are low when they come attacking. The best thing you can do is be well-armed with the Word. You need to have some great Bible verses to throw back in Doubt's face, and before long Doubt will get tired of bothering you and go away.

If you know the Word, you can recognize when Doubt is ringing your doorbell and send him packing. Doubt fills your head with lies because he wants to make you think your faith in Jesus is not enough. You know better, though!

One of my favorite stories, when I'm starting to feel doubt sneak up on me, is the one in Romans 4. It's the story of what happened to Abraham way back in Genesis. Let's look at Abraham's faith and see how that might help us, too.

Abraham's Story

Keep in mind that I'm going to tell you this story in my own words, but you can read the actual account yourself in Romans.

Abraham Believed God

The story starts out with this simple statement—that Abraham believed God (see Romans 4:3). God was so delighted about that, that He gave Abraham some special privileges. Now, just so you're clear about this. Abraham didn't do a lot of great things. He didn't do so many good deeds that God picked him out of a crowd. Therefore, Abraham couldn't really brag about what he did to get God's special blessings. No, Abraham simply *believed* God.

God liked hanging out with Abraham because of Abraham's faith, not his works. So, how did this faith stuff help Abraham?

It meant that Abraham had a relationship with God that was based on things of the heart, soul, and mind. Those are the things we talked about before and the ones that Jesus told us were important to have. Abraham had that very kind of love for God.

The Bible reminds us that faith is the key. God's promise is given to us as a free gift. What was it Abraham had that maintained his faith? What was the promise God made to him?

The Father of Many Nations

Abraham believed God when God told him that he would have a lot of children (see Romans 4:17). He even said that Abraham's children would be as numerous as the stars (verse 18). That had to sound pretty impossible to Abraham. However, Abraham believed that it could happen, even though he was technically too old to be a father. He was already one hundred years old. (And you think *your* dad is old!) Sarah, his wife, was also way past the childbearing years, yet Abraham believed God could do anything (verse 19). If God said he'd have children, then he was pretty sure he would have children (verses 20–21).

Abraham was totally convinced that God could fulfill His promise. Even though Sarah was a little less certain, she remained faithful to her husband. Her husband remained faithful to God, and before the whole thing was over, Isaac was born. Now, that's a pretty powerful baby story, don't you think?

Why This Is a Good Story

I like this story a lot because it reminds me that all things are possible with God. Some things may seem too hard if you don't let God in, but if you do, He can bring about anything that is right for you. This is a great story of what it means not to doubt God.

But what about that Thomas story? Remember "Doubting Thomas?" What can we learn from him? Let's take a look there, too.

Thomas, You Old Doubter, You

You surely know the story of Thomas, the disciple who needed proof that Jesus was alive again before he would believe his friends. Chances are that some of us would need the same proof to believe.

Mary was the first to encounter Jesus after the resurrection. She was the one who told the story of her conversation with Him. Shortly after that, Jesus appeared to His disciples, but Thomas was not present at that meeting. When Thomas came in and they told him the story, Thomas said he could not believe unless he saw the nail wounds in Jesus' hands and the wound in His side. Here's what John 20:26–29 has to say:

> *Eight days later the disciples were together again, and this time Thomas was with them. The doors were locked; but suddenly, as before, Jesus was standing among them. He said, "Peace be with you." Then he said to Thomas, "Put your finger here and see my hands. Put your hand into the wound in my side. Don't be faithless any longer. Believe!"*
>
> *"My Lord and my God!" Thomas exclaimed.*
>
> *Then Jesus told him, "You believe because you have seen me. Blessed are those who haven't seen me and believe anyway." (John 20:26–29 NLT)*

Perhaps the old saying, "Seeing is believing," comes from this very story. Questions will arise often in your walk of faith. Doubts will come around and attack you any chance they get.

What will your answer be? Will you believe anyway? Your Lord and your God must rise each day in your heart, mind, and soul.

Now, Let's Take a Look at That Depression Demon

I sincerely hope that you haven't had to deal with depression yet in your young life. And I pray that you never will. Chances are, though, that you'll be around someone who suffers from serious depression at some time or other. How does depression happen, and how does it take over? How can you overcome its mind-zapping ray gun?

When you start sounding like Eeyore from Winnie the Pooh, when nothing ever seems to go right for you and you're feeling tired and icky all the time, it might be a bit of depression. Depression can make you feel like the weight of the world is on your shoulders, and you don't have answers for anything. The sun goes out, nobody's playing anymore, and everything is gloomy.

In my book for adults, I walked through Psalm 143 to

help them find some ways to overcome the depression demon. We'll use a different Bible translation for you, but let's go through this psalm and see how it can help.

Getting Back to the Light

Step One: Figure Out What
Is Causing the Problem

My enemy has chased me. He has knocked me to the ground. He forces me to live in darkness like those in the grave. —*Psalm 143:3* NLT

What's the problem? He was being attacked by the forces of darkness. He was feeling like everything around him was black and he had no control over what was happening.

When you have a problem and you can't figure out where it is coming from or why you feel so blue, you might want to stop and see if you could be in the middle of spiritual warfare. The battle is going on all the time, and sometimes it can affect you personally.

Step Two: See What the Depression Is Really Doing to You

I am losing all hope; I am paralyzed with fear.

—Psalm 143:4 NLT

Your response to depression is to become fearful and hopeless. You begin to believe that you're simply in the dark and that you can't find your way back to the light.

Step Three: Think About the Things That Make You Feel Good

I remember the days of old. I ponder all your great works. I think about what you have done. —Psalm 143:5 NLT

It may help you to stop if you can and think about the good things God has done for you so far. Think about the loving family He has given you or the good friends you have. Think about the vacation you took last year or the fun you had in Vacation Bible School. Think about the good things.

Step Four: Thank the Lord Anyway!

I reach out for you. I thirst for you as parched land thirsts for rain.   —*Psalm 143:6* NLT

What happens when you're so blue? You want to get things to feel better. You feel dry and thirsty, and you want to have someone take care of your needs. The psalmist says that one choice you have is to "reach out" for the Lord. Look to Him to help you keep believing that He has the answers. Believe that He can fill you up and make you happy again. You can begin that step by thanking Him for all He's done for you in the past.

Remember that Jesus said that He is "living water" (see John 4:10).

Step Five: Ask God to Help You!

Come quickly, LORD, and answer me, for my depression deepens. Don't turn away from me, or I will die.
—*Psalm 143:7* NLT

You see what is happening. You feel like you can't hold on much longer, and you really need help. You're like a person hanging on to a rope for dear life and hoping the rescue squad gets there in time.

When you call on God for help, His rescue crew arrives instantly. He sends the Holy Spirit to comfort and care for you and strengthen you so that you can hold on until things turn around.

Step Six: Listen to What God Wants to Tell You

Let me hear of your unfailing love to me in the morning, for I am trusting you. Show me where to walk, for I have come to you in prayer.   —*Psalm 143:8* NLT

Look at what this is telling you. It says three very important things:

1. You must want more than anything to hear what God would say to you. Your love for Him needs to be your guide.
2. You must trust God to pull you through.
3. You must ask Him to guide your steps and give you direction because that is your prayer.

Step Seven: You Must Pray and Pray Some More

*Save me from my enemies, L*ORD*; I run to you to hide me.*
                                   —*Psalm 143:9* NLT

Look at where the psalmist is putting all of his attention. He is asking God to save him. He is telling the Lord that he wants to be even closer to Him. Imagine a baby chick running to a mother hen, getting shelter under her wing because he's afraid of something in the barnyard.

That's the picture. You can go to the Lord for shelter, and He will protect you. You must keep your eyes on Him as the One who can really help you, and take your eyes off of the problem.

Step Eight: Ask God for Wisdom and Guidance

Teach me to do your will, for you are my God. May your gracious Spirit lead me forward on a firm footing.
—Psalm 143:10 NLT

How many times do we lose our way? How many times do we put all of our worry and energy into the problem at hand, instead of asking God for help?

The psalmist is not only asking God for help, he's saying, "I still need more lessons in doing Your will. I'm still a student. I'm still in need of a teacher. Help me to do Your will because You are my God, You are my personal Savior. I've already committed my heart and mind to You."

Then he ends with a wish, a sort of prayer. He prays

that God's gracious Spirit will lead him forward. He says, "Put me on steady ground, Lord. Keep me safe in You. Help me to land on my feet."

If you have depression demons at your back door, you can keep them away with these steps. If you need help, have your mom or dad or a good friend work through the steps with you. That's why God gave us people to be around us and care for us.

The main thing to remember is that you do have some choices in how you think about things. You have some tools that you can use to help you think better, but these tools will not wipe away all your troubles. If they did, they'd be magic formulas needing a wand, not real-life issues, needing the grace of a heavenly Father. You are a child of God. You always have a place to share your troubles. God will always choose to help you through until you can see the light again.

Chapter 9

Whacko Weeds of Worry (and how to get rid of them!)

L et's say God planted you in a garden. At first, you were a tender little seedling, and He nourished you and gave you just enough to drink and just enough to eat. He brought the sun out so that you could play in the breeze and enjoy the beauty all around you. And then you grew up. Now that you're fully in bloom, you can see the world even better than when you were tiny. Now you start to wonder about everything.

Come to think of it, God did plant the first people in a Garden, and He did just that. He provided everything for them. He gave them all they needed to grow strong and be happy. He was always there for them and loved to watch them enjoy their beautiful surroundings. Then, one day, they, too, started to worry and wonder. Let's go visit Adam and Eve, our first parents, back in Paradise. That's where worry all began.

Planting Worries in the Garden

Genesis 3 gives us the story.

"Now the snake was the most clever of all the wild animals the LORD God had made. One day the snake said to the woman, 'Did God really say that you must not eat fruit from any tree in the garden?'

"The woman answered the snake, 'We may eat fruit from the trees in the garden. But God told us, "You must not eat fruit from the tree that is in the middle of the garden. You must not even touch it, or you will die."'

"But the snake said to the woman, 'You will not die. God knows that if you eat the fruit from that tree, you will learn about good and evil and you will be like God!'

"The woman saw that the tree was beautiful, that its

fruit was good to eat, and that it would make her wise. So she took some of its fruit and ate it. She also gave some of the fruit to her husband, and he ate it."

Then, it was as if their eyes were opened.

—*Genesis 3:1–7*

Never Listen to a Snake!

You may think it's funny that I would actually advise you to never listen to a snake, but times have not really changed. That same snake that tricked Eve in the Garden, tries to trick you, too.

Do you see what he did in the Garden? First, he questioned Eve as though she didn't really understand what God was saying. He acted like he was just asking an innocent question. He caused her to doubt what she knew. He caused her to even doubt what she was told by God Himself.

Step Back!

Step back a moment and think about times when you've started to doubt. Maybe someone poked fun at your faith, or they asked a question that you just didn't have an answer to, and so you started to wonder if you actually knew God as much as you thought. Well, that's kind of what happened to Eve. She started to doubt that she really knew what she should do.

Now, look at what that wily snake does. He goes after her again. He tells her something that he knows will excite her interest. He tries to make himself seem like the one "who *really* knows the answers about God." He casts worry in her mind about the truth.

The Snake Pit

Going back to you: You may have had the experience of someone sharing information with you at school that seemed like the truth. Maybe they told you that your mother doesn't really know what she's talking about when she tells you not to smoke, because smoking isn't really addictive, and you can just enjoy it and look more grown-up. They can make it seem like everything you've been told by someone who loves you and takes care of you is wrong. Now what? They offer you a cigarette, and maybe like Eve, you think, "I'll just try one. It won't be a big deal."

That's why you should never talk to a snake. A snake in any form from Satan himself to a supposed friend at school can just be spreading doubt and worry and trying to trap you into sin. Why do you think a snake crawls on its belly? Why do you think they hide in the dark?

We could get more things from this story, but the main point I want you to see is how doubt and worry can work together to cause you to sin, to go against the things that you know are good.

Keeping Your Face to the Wind

You're at the age where you have to pay attention to standing firm in your beliefs. Your mind will be bombarded with typhoons of information that can seem good, but they will actually be false and angry gods. If you aren't rooted firmly in your faith, you may find yourself being tossed about on other people's ideas. The winds of doubt will blow you in every direction. Before you know it, you'll be totally uprooted because you won't have a foundation anymore. You'll be choked by the weeds of doubt and discontent. Your spirit will dry up. And that's not a very pretty garden to be in.

Finding the Peace Again

Peace of mind is essential to your growth and well-being. You may have noticed how often the Bible writers and disciples greeted each other with a wish for peace. They lived in hard times, and they didn't take for granted the glorious moments when their minds felt free and their hearts were at rest in God.

You shouldn't, either. We're fortunate to live in a culture that allows us freedom of worship and the opportunity to express our faith in God anytime and anyplace. Much of both the ancient world and the modern world is not that blessed. Peace is a gift of God, and one of the benefits of having your heart and mind lined up with God's will.

Peace Is a Fruit of the Spirit

In Galatians 5:22–23, we read about the fruit of the Spirit. Let's look at these verses and see how they can help us when we have anxious or worried minds.

"But the Spirit produces

the fruit of love, joy, peace, patience, kindness, goodness, faithfulness, gentleness, self-control. There is no law that says these things are wrong."

This is like Christmas all year round! God has stacked up presents for you to have anytime, and they are yours free of charge because you are a believer. You can have these anytime you choose to pick them off the tree of His divine love for you. You are part of His garden, attached to the eternal Vine, and so you are always in His care. Look at those gifts. They are so big that He couldn't hide them in a gift box even if He wanted to. They are completely tied with love, and all you have to do is use them.

The one we want to focus on right now, though, is *peace*. You can't have a worried mind and peace at the same time. That just won't happen! You might as well see yourself standing with Eve in the Garden talking to the snake if you're going to give your mind over to worry. Only the Spirit of God can give you peace. That's the only fruit you want to pick.

The Way Worry Helps

Let's make a list of all the ways you've discovered that worry helps your life. Let's see how many times worry has made something better for you. Ready, let's go. Number one is . . .

Okay, we'll come back to that. Number two is, um, oh, yes, here it is . . . it gave you something to do with your mind.

No, it didn't. It took your mind off of praying to the One who could actually help you with your concern. So, scratch that one.

All right, number three is that it gave you something to talk about with your friends. Okay, if negative, "poor-me" talk is really what you need, go with that, but then what? Did you get any answers? Did you find a solution?

Of course, I'm not really talking about conversations where you really are looking for positive and possible ways to deal with a situation that you have already in good faith turned over to God. I'm just talking about those weak chats with friends when you try to outdo each other with how miserable your life is. That's just creating *more* worry!

You get the point—worry doesn't ever offer solutions. It doesn't ever take you to God. It just takes you deeper within yourself and clouds all the issues until you're on your belly like the snake instead of on your knees, where you should be.

So, What's Your Worry Anyway?

Let's look at some more biblical examples of things that cause worry to come in. Isn't it interesting to see how current and relevant the Bible is? We can pull wonderful examples from it to help us with what's going on today in the twenty-first century. Amazing!

Starting with Matthew 6:25, we can see how useless it is to worry about the everyday things in our lives. Jesus says:

So I tell you, don't worry about the food or drink you need to live, or about the clothes you need for your body. Life is more than food, and the body is more than clothes. Look at the birds in the air. They don't plant or harvest or store food in barns, but your heavenly Father feeds them. And you know that you are worth much more than the birds. You cannot add any time to your life by worrying about it.

And why do you worry about clothes? Look at how the lilies in the field grow. They don't work or make clothes for themselves. But I tell you that even Solomon with his riches was not dressed as beautifully as one of these flowers.

God clothes the grass in the field, which is alive today but tomorrow is thrown into the fire. So you can be even more sure that God will clothe you. Don't have so little faith! (verses 25–30)

Your Life Is More Important Than Things!

As you're learning to think about things in new ways, I hope you'll discover that you're already pretty smart. In fact, you may have already noticed that the closer you stick to God, the less you have to worry. The more you try to keep up with the world, the more you can feel dissatisfied with what you have. The truth is that whether or not you have the latest electronic gadget to play music or your own cell phone or the latest fashions, you have more than most of the kids in the world. In fact, just because you have food on the table every day and a place to take a shower when you want to or a cozy place to sleep, you have more than most of the known world.

So What If You Don't Have an iPod?

The only reason to look at that is to get perspective. If you feel like you don't have everything that your best friend has, stop and think about it. Aren't you being provided for in every essential way? Aren't you mightily blessed?

The Bible passage we just noted is a reminder that God has taken care of all of the ones He created, right down to the birds and the flowers. He has made sure that life can be sustained and enjoyed.

You might want to take some time and go watch a few birds. Do they look worried? G. K. Chesterton said that "angels can fly because they take themselves lightly." Sometimes it seems like we need to do that, too. We need to take ourselves lightly and take our faith seriously, and we'll know without a doubt or worry anywhere that everything we really need is taken care of. God has already planned for our good. He has already planned for *your* good.

In fact, He reminds you that you're worth even more than any bird, so why would you worry?

Seek, Look for, Go after, Pursue God!

One of the biggest things to remember any time you are tempted to worry is tied into this verse. It's from that same section of Matthew, verse 33. It says, "The thing you should want most is God's kingdom and doing what God wants. Then all these other things you need will be given to you."

In other words, when you're really looking for God to be number one in your life, and you look for Him in everything you do, and you fill your thoughts with Him, wanting more of what He has to offer, you'll discover that you are at peace. You will discover that you are being taken care of in a big way and that you have no worries at all.

Go on! Look for more of Him and less of the world. You'll start seeing things differently and thinking straight. Those whacko weeds of worry will dry up because they don't belong in your garden, anyway. Now, that's a breath of fresh air!

Tipping over the Worries

If you're still thinking that you just can't help worrying, then let's try to give you something else to do with your time. After all, you might not be able to help worrying, but God can help you if you really want to get past it. Here are some ideas:

Take one day at a time.

Let's say you have a hundred dollars in your "life" bank account for today. You use a little of it, just getting up and getting dressed and prepared for the day. You use some thinking about the test you're having at school or the tryouts for the school play, and so now you have eighty dollars left for the day and it's only 8 A.M.

By 10 A.M., you discover your friend Jenny is mad at you, and you totally forgot to turn in your math paper from when you were out sick last week. Your teacher is somewhat unhappy with you, and now you've got sixty dollars left.

Before noon, you're worrying about how you can get that math paper done when you know your family is going out for the evening. You've still got the history test later in the afternoon, and you're not sure you're prepared for it. You know your dad will be pretty angry if you get another grade that he thinks is less than your best effort. Now the day's not even half over, and you've only got thirty dollars left.

While you're walking home from school, you're worrying so much, you don't see the kid coming at you on the sidewalk on his bike, and you have to jump out of his way, getting your pants all stained when you walked into the lamppost. Nothing is going right today!

Down to Your Last Ten Bucks

Mom tells you to take the dog out for a walk when you get home, and the dog runs off without you. You have to spend time chasing him, and you still have homework to do. Now you're down to only ten dollars left in your life account.

You've literally used up most of your dollars worrying out the day. How can you make a deposit and get things back on track before you are totally spent?

What to Do When You're Spent

Go back through your day. When could you have added to your bank account? When could you have chosen to do something other than worry?

You could have started your day with a prayer. You could have thanked God for being with you through the night and asked for His help with your day as you took the test and went through the tryouts for the play. You could have thanked Him again for helping you and walked out the door with a full bank account.

When you discovered your friend was mad at you, you could have chosen to find out the problem and tried to solve it quickly. You could have set up a time to talk with her and decide how things should be handled. You would have been actively trying to handle the problem rather than simply worrying about it.

Same with the math paper. You could have offered to stay in at lunchtime and finish the paper, or set up a time with your teacher to complete it first thing in the morning or after school. Whatever the solution, you would not have had to worry about it. You would still have a full bank account to spend in more fun ways.

You get the point. You can totally run out of steam to handle things if you spend every moment in worry. Take care of the things you can, and leave the rest to God.

You can speak the Word of God out loud.

If you memorize a few Bible verses in your life, this is one that will help you when you're tempted to worry. It's Philippians 4:6, 7 (NCV), and it says this:

Do not worry about anything, but pray and ask God for everything you need, always giving thanks. And God's peace, which is so great we cannot understand it, will keep your hearts and minds in Christ Jesus.

So, you see the answer. Talk to God, tell Him what you need, and thank Him for caring about you and being with you. You have His Word on it!

Give your cares to God and stand strong.

Worry makes you weaker and weaker. It robs you of your joy and your strength. Look at what 1 Peter 5:6–9 tells you.

Be humble under God's powerful hand so he will lift you up when the right time comes. Give all your worries to him, because he cares about you. Control yourselves and be careful! The devil, your enemy, goes around like a roaring lion looking for someone to eat. Refuse to give in to him, by standing strong in your faith. You know that your Christian family all over the world is having the same kinds of suffering.

This is why it's so important for you to watch what you're thinking. When you're in a weak state, you can be sure the enemy is watching for a chance to come into your life. Stand strong with your family of believers, and you can easily win the battle.

Take a break and rest in God's hand.

Worry is its own activity. It means you're busy stirring up the waters around your life so much that you probably couldn't hear God if He *was* speaking to you to try to help you. Worry is like a loud and obnoxious heavy-metal band. You need to put in ear plugs so you can hear. Worry says all kinds of mean things to you and keeps you paying attention because of its noise.

Pull the Plug on Worry

Stop the music! Pull the plug on worry! Don't listen any-more. Change the CD to something much more soothing that might help you relax. Rest in God's care and grace.

Jesus told you in John 14:27:

I leave you peace; my peace I give you. I do not give it to you as the world does. So don't let your hearts be troubled or afraid.

Jesus did not worry, and you don't have to worry, either!

Make up your mind that worry is a waste of time.

Even after you read this book, you'll probably still worry about things. It seems to be human nature. It doesn't have to be *your* nature, though. You can really choose to think that worry is a waste of time. All these Bible verses are trying to tell you that. When you're tempted to worry, go back and read these verses again and again until they are more important to you than anything you might be worrying about. Make up your mind, and your spirit will be renewed.

Look at Hebrews 13:5. It says:

Keep your lives free from the love of money, and be satisfied with what you have. God has said, "I will never leave you; I will never forget you." So we can be sure when we say, "I will not be afraid, because the Lord is my helper. People can't do anything to me."

Do you see how protected you are? Do you realize that God sees all the details of your life?

Get off the worry train, and get on board the train where the Conductor never leaves you anyplace you don't want to go.

You do your part, and God will do His part. He doesn't want you to carry the load any farther than to His doorstep.

You can depend on Him, and that's a promise!

Chapter 10

Here Comes the Judge

Not Exactly the Olympics

A Little Story: The Judge from Pew Four

It's not always easy to spot them, but the judges are out there all the time. We don't realize how closely they might look at what we do and what we say and what we wear, but it's happening anyway. Let's take a view from the pew that we all can relate to.

You've brought a stranger to church. Your friend does not have a church, so you're excited to have her there. She's dressed in cut-off jeans and is wearing a T-shirt with some kind of peace symbol on it. Her hair is dyed purple. She's sporting a tattoo on her left shoulder.

As you walk into church, the Judge from Pew Four begins the analysis. Hmmm . . . not dressed appropriately for church, obviously a wild girl with that tattoo and purple hair. That's it, the sign goes up, and the judge gives her a 2.0 score as someone who really doesn't belong in this church. Even though she knows you, she's not planning to speak to you this morning. Instead, she holds up her sign of 2.0.

Later in the service, the Judge from Pew Four discovers that your friend is a visiting student from another country. She has come this morning to speak briefly on the topic of freedom and faith and what it is like to be a kid in a country where the freedom to express your faith is not available. She doesn't go to church because it is not allowed in her country. She's bright and shares her faith easily. She laughs at her purple hair and says she just dyed it last night to be sure to get attention because she wanted everyone to hear what she had to say, especially about how much God loves all His children. Everyone enjoys hearing her story.

The Judge in Pew Four tells herself that she knew all along that this girl had to be a good person. She reviews the previous score, and now gives the girl a 10. She feels so pleased with herself that she is such a good JUDGE of character. She holds up her new sign with a 10 on it.

The end.

Whether you're the kid or the Judge in Pew Four, this story goes on all the time. It doesn't go on just in church. It's in every situation you will ever experience. You are always judging and being judged.

The Bible tells us in Matthew:

Don't judge other people, or you will be judged. You will be judged in the same way that you judge others, and the amount you give to others will be given to you. Why do you notice the little piece of dust in your friend's eye, but you don't notice the big piece of wood in your own eye? How can you say to your friend, "Let me take that little piece of dust out of your eye?" Look at yourself! You still have that big piece of wood in your own eye. You hypocrite!

First, take the wood out of your own eye. Then you will see clearly to take the dust out of your friend's eye. (7:1–5)

Let's examine this whole passage and see how we can use it for our own good and everyone else's good, too.

Why Do We Judge Others?

Some of our reasoning may look like this:

- We think someone else just doesn't know the rules . . . our rules, that is!
- We think that we have the answer, and we want to share it.
- We want others to know how smart we are.
- We want others to look up to us.
- We want to feel good about ourselves.
- We believe it's our job to set others straight about things. (That's called "arrogant pride.")
- We think we're providing a needed service.
- We don't stop to think that we could be wrong.
- It's easier to tell others what's wrong with them than it is to take an honest look at ourselves.
- We forgot Rule Number One: Love one another!

No doubt, we could keep this list going, but let's think about some of the points based on what Matthew has to say.

The Two-Edged Sword of Judgment

Right off the bat, we're told to "stop judging others." You're probably thinking that you've always been taught that you should judge others so you can decide if you should make friends with them or not. You think of that as just being wise. Well, we're not really talking about choosing friends here. We're talking about what we sometimes do to both friends and complete strangers alike.

Sending in the Judge

The Bible verse in Matthew is about those moments when we're critical of others in ways that might not be fair. It might be an innocent judgment about someone's hair, their outfit, or their attitude. It's okay to have an opinion and keep it to yourself, but if you feel a need to comment on it to the person or to someone else, the trouble begins. The Bible says, "Don't judge other people, or you will be judged."

Now, that's interesting! Could that mean that as soon as you pass a judgment about how someone looks today, that coming down the hallway is someone who is going to pass that same judgment on *you*?

Suddenly, the judging game is not as much fun. Now, you're not the one who is in the driver's seat, because you lost the game as soon as you started to play. You just became the next person to be judged! The funny part is that no one had a right to do the judging, anyway.

The only One who is qualified to judge is *God*!

You've been taught the "do-unto-others-as-you-would-have-them-do-unto-you" rule. When it comes to how you want them to "do unto you," you're probably impressed with the rule. What about that first part, though? What about your part in how you treat others? What score would you give yourself on that?

Getting the Log Out

The thing to look at when judging others is all about how we "see" others.

We Need New Glasses!

We think someone else's little problem needs to be corrected by us, because we don't want anyone to notice we have a *big* problem ourselves. We're blind to our own faults.

We give ourselves excuses to behave badly. But in

Romans 2, the Bible says that we have no excuse or even a defense for our behavior when we judge others, because we do the same things ourselves. That log is jammed in our eyes, and we can't see ourselves. Take a moment and imagine that log jammed into your eye. Can you see anything?

Log Jams

Have you ever noticed that when you're in a good mood, the world looks much brighter? You're nicer to the people around you, more forgiving, kinder? You don't need others to be just like you.

What happens when you're in some pickle about something, and you're just sour all the way around? Then you think everyone should see things your way, you see only the bad things in those around you, you think the world is out to get you. That's when you're heading for a log jam. That's when you're not even able to feel or see the judge that lurks within you.

Having Good Judgment

Please understand that in this whole chapter about judgment, we're not talking about having good judgment. We're not talking about the things you know that you should do to be safe and to be careful of yourself and others. We're talking about the things that are triggered in your mind that give you an excuse to think bad thoughts about other people.

The battle for your mind is constant, and if it's not piling up logs in one way, it goes at it in another. Walking into a room at school wearing your long black robe and pounding your gavel is not helping you make friends or share the love of God. It's only setting you up as someone other kids will want to run away from.

How Do You Keep the Judge Away?

- You stop making excuses for your behavior.
- You take another look at yourself.

■ You look for the *good* in others.

■ You ask God to show you what *you* need to understand about the way you're thinking.

■ You check your heart and your "love meter" to see if your thinking is coming from the right place.

■ You look at your trust level for others and see if you need to change some things.

■ You look at your friendships and try to be kinder.

■ You give God the thanks for being the One who handles all the stuff you don't understand about other people.

■ You give up your need to let others know how "right" you are.

■ You take the log out of your own eye first.

Seeing More Clearly

You've been blessed. You are a child of God. Look at what the Bible says in 2 Peter 1:5–9 NCV:

Because you have these blessings, do your best to add these things to your lives: to your faith, add goodness; and to your goodness, add knowledge; and to your knowledge, add self-control; and to your self-control, add patience; and to your patience, add service for God; and to your service for God, add kindness for your brothers and sisters in Christ; and to this kindness, add love. If all these things are in you and are growing, they will help you to be

*useful and productive in your knowledge of our Lord
Jesus Christ. But anyone who does not have these things
cannot see clearly. He is blind and has forgotten that he
was made clean from his past sins.*

Taking the log out of your own eye will help you see
more clearly. Taking a moment to think before you cast
judgment on anyone else will help you be more loving
and kind. You are growing in the Lord every day. Let
your heart guide your thoughts and keep you always in
His love.

Be Kind to Yourself, Too

Remember, too, that as you think good thoughts about
others, it's okay to think good thoughts about yourself, as
well. Talking nicely to yourself is a loving thing to do.
Sometimes the judge in you is way too hard on yourself.
If you find that is happening, go back and apply all the
tools you would use to be kinder to others and use them
for you. That will help you see things more clearly. You
may discover the log has disappeared.

Chapter 11

Change Your Mind and Your Socks!

Hey, Are We There Yet?

You've probably been on a few trips with your parents that seemed to go on and on. Maybe you got stuck in traffic or the scenery was just not that impressive and even after taking a nap, you find that you still haven't reached your destination. Finally, you can't stand it, and you call up to the driver, "Are we there yet?"

The Children of Israel Ask, "Are We There Yet?"

Now, step back in history and try to imagine the children of Israel as they wandered around on their way to the Promised Land. Unlike you, they didn't have a chest packed with ice, sandwiches, and lemonade. They didn't even have their choice of fifteen fast-food restaurants at every exit. Instead, they had the hot desert, worn-out sandals, and manna and quail to keep them alive and well. A little different scene, but some little kid riding a donkey for over two years probably wondered, "Are we there yet?"

Trouble is, they *weren't* there! In fact, they drove their herds around for forty years, and most of them never did get there. The whole trip should have taken them eleven days, but it took them forty years (see Deuteronomy 1:2). You have to wonder what they were thinking!

Anyway, the point is that you will have some wilderness experiences in your life. You may even have some wilderness thinking going on right now. What are you going to do about it? Imagine if you're ten years old now as you read this book, and if it takes you forty years to understand God's direction, you'll be fifty before you even start to get on course. Whoa! Don't let that happen to you!

Let's do some wilderness training right now. That is the training it takes to keep you out of the wilderness in your own life.

What Is Wilderness Thinking?

In some ways, wilderness thinking is "stuck" thinking. It's where you can't see another way to go no matter where you look. God finally had to speak to the children of Israel. He said, "You have stayed at this mountain long enough. It is time to break camp and move on" (Deuteronomy 1:6–7 NLT).

Can you think of any time when God might say that to you? "Look, you've walked around your reason for being mad at your friend long enough, move on." Or, "You've kept your worries to yourself long enough, let's talk about them!" You see, you can get stuck in "stinkin' thinkin'." You can be in a place that your mind has no business being and just sit there like a lump of clay waiting to be tossed in the furnace. Stop! It's time to move on.

Let's get out of the wilderness as quickly as possible.

Getting Closer to the Promised Land

Pretend you're going to do an oil painting in your art class at school. The teacher has given you the freedom to paint anything you want as long as it means something to you and it's something you'll be proud to put in the school fine-arts show. Let's also assume that you love to paint, and this is really an exciting opportunity for you.

How do you start? Chances are, before you begin to draw or paint anything, you start with a vision, a plan. You think about all the subjects you might like to paint. Maybe you'll paint the backyard scenery behind your house, or try to copy an old photograph of your great-aunt Jessie. You start by thinking clearly about what you want to do. You cannot create anything, much less a masterpiece, without a plan.

Are You Ready to Paint?

Maybe, or maybe not! You have a great idea, but now doubt has come into your head. You're pretty sure you're not a very good artist and you won't be able to do it. You set your mind up for failure. You start to complain that you don't have the right paint colors and your brush is not very good. You tell yourself that you can't possibly do this.

Are you starting to hear the children of Israel complaining in the background? Can you hear them whining that they should have just stayed in Egypt because now they aren't so sure they can make it?

What's Your Mind-set?

If you start with a mind-set that says you can't do it, guess what? You won't be able to do it! That's right! If you want to do anything *ever,* you have to believe that it is something you can do. God has given you many gifts, and He wants you to use them. He believes you can paint.

If you start grumbling and complaining and becoming miserable over your painting, your vision will fade. You will forget what you wanted to do because you will be taking your eyes off the goal. You'll just be looking at what isn't perfect and getting more gray skies than blue. You'll live up to your own expectation that you can't do it.

Step past your painting for a moment and look at life in general. How do you get out of wilderness thinking about anything in life?

Steps to Try:

- Create a plan.
- Believe in your ability to carry out the plan.
- Have an attitude of gratitude.
- Think about where you're going, *not* where you've been.
- Look for God's help and guidance.
- Remind yourself of your first idea, your plan.
- Get the job done!

Changing Your Mind Is Like Changing Your Socks . . . Sort Of!

If you've ever been in the same room with someone who didn't change their socks for a day or two or maybe longer, you may have noticed a certain ugly smell in the air. You may have even been tempted to ask, "What stinks?" Stinky socks are not unlike stinky thoughts. You need to change both of them as fast as possible.

The Stinky Sock Wars

Let's say your brother just came in from playing basketball in the hot sun and he's all sweaty. He takes off his cross-trainers, and the most horrible smell whips across the room and hits you right in the nose. You suggest rather loudly that he should go change his socks or maybe take a shower. It seems very reasonable. But . . . he doesn't feel like it right then.

Somebody Do It for Me!

He looks at you and says, "Hey, if it bothers you so much, go get me some clean socks and take these stinky ones to the laundry room. I don't feel like doing it right now."

You know if you do it, things will be more pleasant for you, but there's no way you're touching those smelly socks. So, you decline and keep complaining. You finally take the issue to a higher court. You complain to Mom.

Those Wilderness Children

The children of Israel did the same thing. When things didn't go their way, they complained to Moses. Moses said prayers for them. He kept asking God to help them, but God was getting a little upset with the lazy children for not appreciating anything He'd already done for them. He expected them to be responsible to do the job at hand.

He expects the same thing of you! When your mind is cluttered with things that need to be changed or washed or tossed out completely, you need to get ready for a new mind-set. You've got to be responsible for what you think. You might stay a wilderness child if you don't.

God Will Lead You Forward

God will lead you, guide you, and tell you what direction to go, but you need to do the walking. He can't do it all for you. You have an important part to play yourself. Whether you're making some new decisions because you've been stuck on old ones, or whether you're creating a new plan for your life, you need to take the action steps yourself. Only you can paint that masterpiece. Without your brush, the canvas remains blank.

Putting It Off Till Later

In our previous little story of your brother with the stinky socks, we saw the reason why putting something off till later is not a very good answer. When you're tempted to do that, maybe you should picture those smelly socks sitting right next to you. You know that means you'd have to do something—even if it's just to get away from the smell.

The Time Is *Now*!

When you're trying to do something as difficult as changing your mind, you might be tempted to put it aside until tomorrow. Then, you might think that it can't hurt to wait a few more days. Lots of people do that about prayer. They mean to pray—they just never seem to find the time. The time is *now*!

Whatever it is that needs to be changed when you're out there in the desert, it needs to be changed right away. You're already thirsty. You know when you're hot and thirsty and the ice-cream truck starts playing its music as it comes down your street. What happens if you don't run right away and grab your dollar for a cone? That's right, the truck goes on without you.

You Missed the Ice-Cream Truck

The same thing can happen in other areas of life, too. You can wait too long, and the chance to change things will pass you by. You'll have to wait a long time, and an eleven-day journey can end up taking you forty years. Your ice-cream cone will melt.

If you keep your allowance in a jar in your room and you know it's okay for you to get ice cream when the truck comes by, then you're pre- pared and ready to dip that cone in chocolate sauce. If you haven't planned ahead, you still might not be ready, even if you see the truck coming. God wants you to always be ready to receive the gifts He has for you.

In my book for grown-ups, I give them ten different ways that they can be having a hard time with "stinkin' thinkin'." The list tries to show the ways we talk to ourselves and to others when we're not thinking very well. I've changed it a little bit for you.

The Stinkin' Thinkin' List

1. It's too late to change my future!
2. I want someone else to take care of it!
3. Everything is just too hard!
4. I can't help it—I'm just a kid!
5. I want it *now*!

6. It's not *my* fault!
7. Poor me! Poor me!
8. God doesn't really love me!
9. Other kids have more than I do!
10. I'll do it my way!

Did I miss any of the excuses you use to stay stuck? If I did, you can add them to the list yourself.

We'll look at one more wilderness thought, and then go on. One of the biggest roadblocks to ever winning at life is the one that says, "Everything is too hard, and so I think I'll give up!" Did you ever use that one?

Breaking Those Bad Habits

We'll pretend that you like pink bubble gum and you have been told over and over again by your teachers and your parents that you can't chew gum all the time. You've agreed to work on remembering the rule about gum chewing. What happens?

It Gets Harder to Remember!

Suddenly, it's like everyone you know is offering you bubble gum. They tell you to just keep it till later, but

you never do. You pop it in your mouth and forget it's there. Your teacher sees it, remembers the rule, and makes you write one hundred times that you won't chew gum in school. You have to have your parents sign the paper when you're done. It just got harder.

You tell your parents, "It's just too hard," and you want to give up. You lose your courage to even try. You lose what the Bible calls your "heart." But, think again.

Romans 5:3–5 says:

We also have joy with our troubles, because we know that these troubles produce patience. And patience produces character, and character produces hope. And this hope will never disappoint us, because God has poured out his love to fill our hearts.

So, don't lose heart, don't give up . . . hang tough! You can clean up your act, change your mind, and change your socks any time you're ready. You can do it because God will help you!

Don't be a whiner! Be a winner!

Chapter 12

Fix Your Thoughts, Don't Fix the Blame!

You probably don't do this, but some people like to make excuses for why they made a bad choice. They come up with reasons why they didn't listen to their parents or get their homework done or go to piano practice. They ignore the fact that God is even part of their lives.

Our goal in this chapter is to give you some tools to help fix the problems that come up in your life without fixing the blame on others. If you can learn to fix your thoughts on the truth of the Holy Spirit, then you won't be tempted to make excuses. Let's take a look at some all-too-human examples from the Word.

Finding Someone Else to Blame

God knows us so well. This goes all the way back to our first family in the Garden. The first people to get caught doing something they were specifically told *not* to do, handled it by fixing the blame. Let's look at Adam's response when God was trying to find them in the Garden.

"But the Lord God called to the man and said, 'Where are you?' The man answered, 'I heard you walking in the garden, and I was afraid because I was naked, so I hid.'

"God asked, 'Who told you that you were naked? Did you eat fruit from the tree from which I commanded you not to eat?'

"The man said, 'You gave this woman to me and she gave me fruit from the tree, so I ate it.'

"Then the Lord God said to the woman, 'How could you have done such a thing?'

"She answered, 'The snake tricked me, so I ate the fruit.'"
Genesis 3:9–13

Hey, It Wasn't My Fault!

Do you see what happened? No one took personal responsibility for their actions. They instantly blamed each other. Adam blamed God because God had given him the woman. Then he blamed the woman because she gave him the fruit. Eve blamed the snake because she felt tricked by the whole thing. What was the result? They felt naked before God. In other words, they felt like God could see right through them.

Have you ever been caught in a moment where you weren't telling the whole truth and nothing but the truth? If so, you might know what that feels like. They were ashamed of themselves, but they couldn't even admit it.

God aLways Loves you!

One more point to make in this story is this: God was angry with Adam and Eve for what they did. However, just a bit further down in Genesis, we read that even though God punished them, He also immediately started to help them. He made clothes for them and provided for their needs.

The point is that, even when you sin, God forgives and works with you to help you not sin again. That can only happen when you admit the truth, fix your eyes and heart on Him, and work with Him to work things out.

The Excusonator!

Whenever you find yourself in a tight spot, by something you've done or maybe even left undone, your mind races to find a way out. Like Adam and Eve, you run for the bushes, hoping not to be discovered. That's when the Excusonator shows up. It always makes you feel better to do wrong if you have a reason you can give for wrong behavior. It's how we trick ourselves and how Satan tricks us, too.

What Kinds of Excuses Do We Give?

- I did it because my friend did it!
- No one told me I couldn't do it!
- I don't feel good!
- I couldn't help it!
- I didn't think it was such a big deal!
- All my friends do it!
- I saw Dad do it!
- Everybody wants me to be like my sister!
- The dog chewed my homework paper!
- The alarm didn't go off on time!
- Everybody else gets to do it!
- I had too much sugar!
- Mom didn't remind me!
- I'm just a kid!
- So, I made a mistake . . . sue me!

I love the last one because that seems to dismiss any wrong at all. The point is, you can add to this list of excuses, or you can start taking responsibility for your actions. Just because the blame game is played all the time, doesn't mean you have to become the champion. You can even stop playing.

How Do You Stop the Blame Game?

- ▣ You can come out of the bushes. You don't need to hide from yourself or from God.
- ▣ You can face the truth. You can look at yourself in the mirror and admit what you did wrong. You can be the one to own the wrong.
- ▣ You can check to see how you really feel about what you did wrong. If you're sad about it and wish you had not done it, you can . . .
- ▣ Turn to God and ask His forgiveness. You don't have to give Him your old excuses because He's not interested in "why" you did it. He's interested in what you want to do now to make amends. He's interested in what your heart has learned.
- ▣ You can accept God's forgiveness and ask for His help in not allowing you to do that kind of wrong again. That's part of what we ask every day in the Lord's Prayer.
- ▣ If you've hurt someone in your wrongdoing, you can now go to that person and ask them to forgive you. Sometimes you might even need to try to make amends like replacing a broken or stolen item.

If you're not that familiar with the Lord's Prayer, it goes like this:

Jesus said to his followers, "Your Father knows the

things you need before you ask him." So when you pray, you should pray like this:

Our Father in heaven,
may your name always be kept holy.
May your kingdom come
and what you want be done,
here on earth as it is in heaven.
Give us the food we need for each day.
Forgive us for our sins,
just as we have forgiven those who sinned against us.
And do not cause us to be tempted,
but save us from the Evil One.
Matthew 6:8–13

When your mind is not sure what to do, stop first and pray this prayer. God will help you before you make a mistake.

Also, in John 8:32, Jesus said, "If you continue to obey my teaching, you are truly my followers. Then you will know the truth, and the truth will make you free."

How Can Truth Set You Free?

What does it mean to be free of something? Anything? Let's think of examples:

- If you don't have homework after school, you're free to go play.
- If you finish your chores at home, you're free to watch TV.
- If you ask someone to forgive you and they do, your heart feels better.
- If you admit something to yourself that wasn't really true, you're free to discover what the truth really is.
- If you have time to yourself, you're free to choose how to spend it.

After being set free, you will be able to look back and see how certain things were working in your mind to keep you captured. You're free to explore, to rejoice, to sing, to celebrate, to play, to work, to give, to receive. Freedom comes with a variety of gifts.

Being set free means that you don't always know you're free or that you've got things working in your mind to keep you captured. Your own mind can be a prison, and it can make you a slave. You can think in such a way that you have no freedom at all. That's usually the time when you've allowed the Excusonator to come in and live there, or Satan is trying to trick you, or you just don't know the truth.

The truth sets you free! Clap your hands, stamp your feet, jump for joy! You're free! Every time you embrace the truth, let it guide you, and let it lead you, you're free. God is truth, and He will always set you free!

Doing It *Your* Way!

One final thing I'd really like you to think about is this: You live in a world today that applauds you if you do things your own way. You get credit for being first or best or smartest. All of those things are fine, but sometimes they cause you to forget another truth. That truth is that you belong to God and not to yourself.

Psalm 78:4–8 NLT says:

We will not hide these truths from our children but will tell
the next generation about the glorious deeds of the LORD.
We will tell of his power and the mighty miracles he did.
For he issued a decree to Jacob; he gave his law to Israel. He
commanded our ancestors to teach them to their children,
so the next generation might know them—even the children
not yet born—that they in turn might teach their children.

So each generation can set its hope anew on God,
remembering his glorious miracles and obeying his com-
mands. Then they will not be like their ancestors—stubborn,
rebellious, and unfaithful, refusing to give their hearts to
God.

God wants you to have a very positive attitude. He
wants you to know all the good things He has planned for
your life. He wants you to give your heart and mind and
soul to Him so that He can favor your life with good things.
He wants your thoughts to be directed toward Him in
everything you do.

A Prayer for You

Please pray this prayer with me that God will protect your
heart and mind and help you be a winner on the battle-

field for your thoughts. Now is such a great time to learn how to be strong so you can win the battle your whole life through. You will always have my prayers for you.

Dear Lord,
Please watch over (put your name here). Please strengthen his/her heart and mind toward You. Please help him/her win the battle. Bless all that he/she does to learn more about You and to grow in spirit according to Your will and Your mercy. Praise You, Lord, today for this wonderful kid. Bless him/her with loving and obedient thoughts every day. Amen.

Isaiah 55:6–9 NLT reminds us about how the Lord thinks and what He wants from you. Let's take a look:

"Seek the LORD while you can find him. Call on him now while he is near. Let the people turn from their wicked deeds. Let them banish from their minds the very thought of doing wrong! Let them turn to the LORD that he may have mercy on them. Yes, turn to our God, for he will abundantly pardon.

"'My thoughts are completely different from yours,' says the LORD. 'And my ways are far beyond anything you could imagine. For just as the heavens are higher than the earth, so are my ways higher than your ways and my thoughts higher than your thoughts.'"

Have Good Thoughts!

May all your thoughts build you up and make you smile before the Lord. Be His kid in every way you think and every way you act. If you do, He will bless you forever.

Thanks for sharing this book with me. My prayers, my thoughts, and my heart are with you.

Joyce Meyer

JOYCE MEYER has been teaching the Word of God since 1976 and in full-time ministry since 1980. She is the best-selling author of more than seventy inspirational books, including *Approval Addiction*, *In Pursuit of Peace*, *How to Hear from God*, and *Battlefield of the Mind*. She has also released thousands of audio teachings as well as a complete video library. Joyce's *Enjoying Everyday Life®* radio and television programs are broadcast around the world, and she travels extensively conducting conferences. Joyce and her husband, Dave, are the parents of four grown children and make their home in St. Louis, Missouri.

To contact the author in the United States:
Joyce Meyer Ministries
P.O. Box 655
Fenton, Missouri 63026
(636) 349-0303
www.joycemeyer.org

Please include your testimony or help received from this book when you write. Your prayer requests are welcome.
To contact the author in Canada:
Joyce Meyer Ministries-Canada, Inc.
Lambeth Box 1300
London, ON N6P 1T5
(636) 349-0303

To contact the author in Australia:
Joyce Meyer Ministries-Australia
Locked Bag 77
Mansfield Delivery Centre
Queensland 4122
07 3349 1200

To contact the author in England:
Joyce Meyer Ministries
P.O. Box 1549
Windsor
SL4 1GT
Great Britain
(0) 1753-831102

OTHER BOOKS BY JOYCE MEYER

Battlefield of the Mind *

Battlefield of the Mind Devotional

Approval Addiction

Ending Your Day Right

In Pursuit of Peace

The Secret Power of Speaking God's Word

Seven Things That Steal Your Joy

Starting Your Day Right

Beauty for Ashes Revised Edition

How to Hear from God *

Knowing God Intimately

The Power of Forgiveness

The Power of Determination

The Power of Being Positive

The Secrets of Spiritual Power

The Battle Belongs to the Lord

The Secrets to Exceptional Living

Eight Ways to Keep the Devil Under Your Feet

Teenagers Are People Too!

Filled with the Spirit

Celebration of Simplicity

* Study Guide available for this title

The Joy of Believing Prayer

Never Lose Heart

Being the Person God Made You to Be

A Leader in the Making

"Good Morning, This Is God!"

Jesus—Name Above All Names

Making Marriage Work
(Previously published as
Help Me—I'm Married!)

Reduce Me to Love

Be Healed in Jesus' Name

How to Succeed at Being Yourself

Weary Warriors, Fainting Saints

Life in the Word Devotional

Be Anxious for Nothing *

Straight Talk Omnibus

Don't Dread

Managing Your Emotions

Healing the Brokenhearted

Me and My Big Mouth! *

Prepare to Prosper

Do It Afraid!

Expect a Move of God in Your Life . . . Suddenly!

*Enjoying Where You Are on the Way to
Where You Are Going*

The Most Important Decision You Will Ever Make

When, God, When?

Why, God, Why?

The Word, the Name, the Blood

Tell Them I Love Them

Peace

The Root of Rejection

If Not for the Grace of God *

JOYCE MEYER SPANISH TITLES

*Las Siete Cosas Que Te Roban el Gozo
(Seven Things That Steal Your Joy)*

*Empezando Tu Día Bien
(Starting Your Day Right)*

BOOKS BY DAVE MEYER

Life Lines

Check out the entire
BATTLEFIELD of the MIND
family of books!

Battlefield of the Mind

If you suffer from negative thoughts, Joyce Meyer can help. With her million-copy bestseller, Joyce Meyer shows how you can change your life by simply changing your mind. Gain control over your mind, learn to be patient, and conquer the damaging thoughts that influence your life every day.

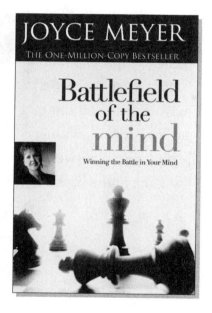

Battlefield of the Mind
Study Guide

The thought-provoking questions in this companion study guide will help you search for truths that you can apply to your life immediately. Ideal for individual and group use, the workbook format provides space to fill in answers to each question, and you can check your work with the special answer section in the back.

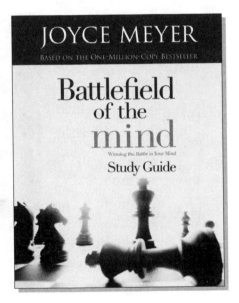

Battlefield of the Mind
Devotional

This devotional offers short, powerful, and relevant messages you can read from day to day. The readings will help you identify the distorted thoughts of the enemy, effectively confront them, and find victory in transforming your thinking. Each reading offers you strength, encouragement, and most importantly, triumph in the battlefield!

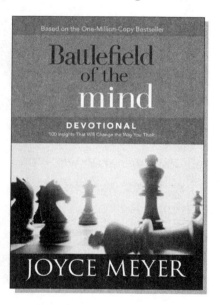

Battlefield of the Mind
for Teens

Joyce Meyer partners with popular author and speaker Todd Hafer to bring her respected wisdom and sound advice to today's teens—a group that desperately needs to hear Joyce's message. Using contemporary language, well-timed humor, powerful statistics, and teen-appropriate applications and calls to action, this book offers teens a relevant and engaging version of the bestselling original.

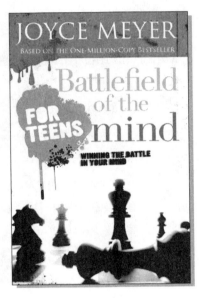

Battlefield of the Mind
for Kids

Partnering with Karen Moore, Joyce Meyer provides the same inspiring message of encouragement and hope as the original edition for adults, but in a manner specifically geared for children. Written in an upbeat style and filled with interesting stories and illustrations, this book will appeal to these readers at a time when they need it most—their preteen years.

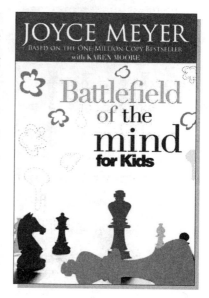